AF540202

GRASSROOTS DEVELOPMENT INITIATIVES IN INDIA

Rights Based Approach to Development and Advocacy

GRASSROOTS DEVELOPMENT INITIATIVES IN INDIA

Rights Based Approach to Development and Advocacy

Sampat Kale

GRASSROOTS DEVELOPMENT INITIATIVES IN INDIA:
Rights Based Approach to Development and Advocacy

Sampat Kale

First Published 2015

ISBN 978-93-5002-355-6 (Hb)

Published by
AAKAR BOOKS
28 E Pocket IV, Mayur Vihar Phase I, Delhi 110 091
Phone : 011 2279 5505 Telefax : 011 2279 5641
aakarbooks@gmail.com; www.aakarbooks.com

Printed at
Sapra Brothers, Delhi 110 092

Contents

List of Tables

List of Illustrations

LIST OF MAPS

Foreword

The preamble to the Constitution of India expounds on the objectives of securing justice, liberty, equality, and fraternity. To achieve these objectives, a number of provisions have been made for the upliftment of scheduled castes, scheduled tribes, and other disadvantaged sections. In a speech delivered in the Constituent Assembly of India on November 25, 1949, B.R. Ambedkar raised a couple of questions: "How long shall we continue to live this life of contradictions? How long shall we continue to deny equality in our social and economic life?" Further, he said: "We must remove this contradiction at the earliest possible moment......" With this background, this book deals with the rights of tribals.

To remove the contradictions between the objectives of social and economic equality and the status of tribals, the Government of India allocated funds for tribal development under the Five Year Plans. Moreover, the Government of India notified 15 districts of Maharashtra, for the administration of tribal areas. The government employs its administrative machinery for implementing the tribal development programmes. Nevertheless, the Government of India acknowledged its failure, and under the Ministry of Tribal Affairs, made programmes for the promotion of voluntary action in the area of tribal development.

This study tackles the conscientising role of voluntary organisations, viz. the Vidhayak Sansad and the Shramajivi Sanghatana in Thane district of Maharashtra. The founders of both organisations believed in the ideologies of socialism and social justice. They had strong commitment to work for the

Adivasis' socio-economic development.

For examining the role of the selected voluntary organisations, Dr. Sampat Kale used Paulo Freire's conscientisation—a conceptual framework. It refers to the process of awakening "to perceive social, political and economic contradictions, and to take action against the oppressive elements of reality." Coincidentally, the leaders of the voluntary organisations, the then ministers, the then top government bureaucrats, and the then chief justice of India were progressives, who contributed to wage the struggle to resolve the contradictions in which the *Adivasis* were caught. The study, therefore, underlines the importance of the avant-garde.

S.M. DAHIWALE

Acknowledgements

This book focuses on the grassroots development initiatives and role of conscientisation in empowerment of *adivasis* and other marginalised sections of society through the rights based approach to development by the Vidhayak Sansad and the Shramjeevi Sanghatana in Thane district of Maharashtra state.

The book evolved from the Ph.D. thesis titled, *Development Initiatives with Special Reference to Vidhayak Sansad and Shramajeevi Sanghatana, Thane District of Maharashtra State* submitted to the University of Pune, and is an outcome of my long-term association with both the organisations and studies done while working with these organisations. It would not have been possible for me to complete the book without the able guidance and support of Dr. S.M. Dahiwale. I thank him for the foreword and his constant encouragement and the unfailing patience with which he read my thesis drafts.

I extend my sincere thanks to Dr. Sanjeevanee Mulay (Gokhale Institute of Politics and Economics, Pune) who has been the source of inspiration for my research work and the book. Her vast experience in research has helped me in data collection and carrying out further analysis. I am grateful to Dr. Shirish Kavadi and Ms. Anuradha Gupte for review of the manuscript and providing valuable editorial support. I am also thankful to Mr. K.K. Saxena of Aakar Books, Delhi for publishing this book.

At the Tata Institute of Social Sciences, Mumbai I would like to thank Prof. S. Parasuraman, Director, for his immense support for completing this book. I am thankful to Prof. Abdul Shaban, Deputy Director, Tuljapur Campus, for his motivation and constant encouragement for writing papers, articles, and particularly this book. I am also thankful to Prof. Rohit Jain, Prof. Ramesh Jare, Prof. M. Kunhaman, and Prof. Shahaji Narwade who have been a sources of motivation in writing the book.

At the National Centre for Advocacy Studies, Pune, I would like to thank Mr. John Samuel, President. I am also grateful to Amitabh Behar, Vijaya Patnekar, Gnana Prakasam, Pankaj Bedi, and Rifat Mumtaz for their support in debate and discussions.

At the Vidhayak Sansad and Shramjeevi Sanghatana, Thane, I am thankful to the founders Mr. Vivek Pandit and Mrs. Vidyullata Pandit who enabled me to learn from grassroots concerns and also for spending their valuable time for discussion during my fieldwork. For this study I received immense help from various activists as well. I sincerely thank Mr. Pradip Khairkar, Mr. Keshav Nankar, Mr. Suresh Renjad, Mr. Balaram Bhoir, the late Mr. Janubhau, Mrs. Venutai Meghwale, Mr. Kisan Chaure, Dalvi Guruji, Mr. Nana Mogare and many others. I would also like to thank Mr. Vijay Bhati and Vinayak Malgaonkar for providing the photographs.

I sincerely thank the Department of Sociology, University of Pune, Gokhale Institute of Politics and Economics, Pune, and the National Centre for Advocacy Studies, Pune, for their library facilities.

At the Savitribai Phule Pune University, Pune I take this opportunity to thank the late Prof. Sharmila Rege, who was the Head of the Department of Sociology then, and Dr. Vidyut Bhagwat, who was the Head of the Krantijyoti Savitribai Phule Women's Studies Centre then, for their support and encouragement. I thank my friends, Mr. Taj Ladaf who helped me in data collection in the field and Mr. Nandkumar Mete. Their constant support and motivation has helped me in completing the book.

My parents, wife, and my sons Jaydev and Malhar provided enormous support which enabled me to participate in a number of fieldwork activities and meetings to complete this book. My wife, Medha provided immense support and has been the source of encouragement in all my achievements. I am also grateful to Mr. Ajay Mulay for his constant support and motivation to complete the book.

March 21, 2015 **Sampat Chandrabhan Kale**

1

Development Initiatives: Theoretical Framework

I. THE ARGUMENT

Over the period of the past sixty-five years, the journey of independent India presents a mixed but depressing picture of excluded, deprived, and marginalised people with little or no access to basic rights or a life with dignity. The hegemonic political culture of India systematically institutionalised this marginalisation and exclusion. In order to make democracy more meaningful and substantive for the marginalised groups and communities like the ex-untouchables, *adivasis*,[1] and women, initiatives in the form of legislations, developmental actions, and social movements were made by the state and civil society. Unfortunately, the attempt at democratic decentralisation of the Indian polity and society failed due to its top-down policy planning and development approach that bottom up approach in planning and implementation of the poverty reduction programmes. This failure explains the persistence of widespread economic and social inequality. It also reflects the extensive nature of human deprivations: denial of basic rights and the absence of freedoms. Illiteracy, ill health, malnutrition, insufficient earnings, social exclusion, and lack of say in decision-making must all be viewed as a 'set of un-freedom constituting human poverty'.[2]

As the subject matter of the study is to examine the results of the developmental programmes envisaged for the *adivasis*, it is necessary to take an overview of some important findings since the adoption of the Constitution of India in 1949.

India has the largest *adivasi* population in the world. According to the 2011 census, India has the largest *adivasi* population in the world. According to the 2011 census, the *adivasi* population of India is 10,42,81,034 persons, constituting 8.6 per cent of the population of the country. As per the census of India 2011, the number of individual groups notified as Scheduled Tribes is 705.[3] The Anthropological Survey of India under the People of India Project identified as many as 461 *adivasi* communities in the country. The *adivasi* population of the country, as per the 2001 census, is 84.51 million constituting 8.14 per cent of the total population.[4] In 2001, their number was around 820 lakh persons. They are divided into two categories: (1) frontier tribes and (2) non-frontier tribes. Frontier tribes are from northeast India. They constitute 11% of the total tribal population.. The remaining states and union territories are known as non-frontiers constituting 89% of the total tribal population.[5] More than half the Scheduled Tribe population is concentrated in the states of Madhya Pradesh, Chhattisgarh, Maharashtra, Orissa, Jharkhand, and Gujarat. *Adivasi* communities live in about 15% of the country's areas in various ecological and geo-climatic conditions ranging from plains, forest hills, and inaccessible areas. As compared to the sex ratio for the overall population (933 female per 1,000 male), the sex ratio among the *adivasis* is slightly higher at 977 females per 1,000 males (2001 Census).

The following section gives an outline of policies and programmes for the development of *adivasis*.

State-wise Tribal Population Percentage in India

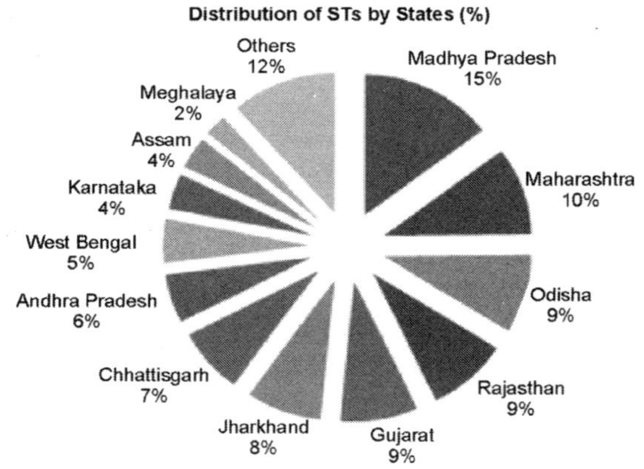

State-wise Tribal Population Percentage in India

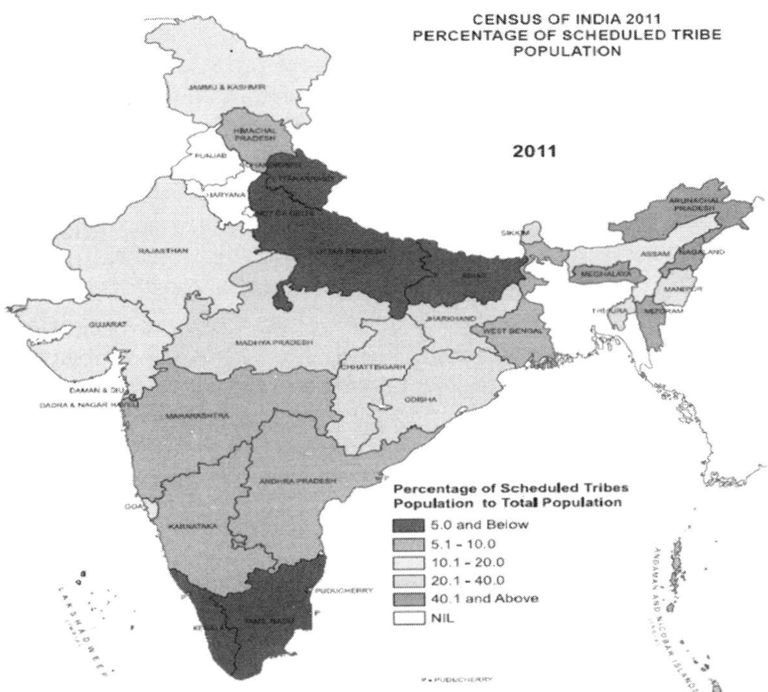

Source: *Census of India 2011*, percentage of Scheduled Tribe population, Tribal profile at a glance, May 2013, www.tribal.nic.in

I.1 Policies and Programmes for the Development of *Adivasis* in India

Until 1919, the tribals were termed as depressed classes. Later, in the 1931 census, they were classified as 'primitive tribes'. The 1941 census described them as 'tribes', and the 1951 census referred to them as 'Scheduled Tribes'.[6]

In a circular fashion, tribes are defined as those groups enumerated as tribes under the Indian Constitution. Thus, Article 366(25) of the Constitution defines Scheduled Tribes as follows:

Scheduled Tribes means such tribes or tribal communities or parts of or groups within such tribes or tribal communities as are deemed

under Article 342 to be Scheduled Tribes for the purposes of this Constitution.[7]

The term 'Scheduled Tribes' was inserted in the Constitution vide Article 342 (1). Since the adoption of the Constitution, the Scheduled Tribes are considered important in all government policies and programmes. Therefore, in all Five Year Plans, the government has allocated funds for tribal development. The First Five Year Plan allotted additional financial resources to address the problems of *adivasi* people rather than evolving a well-defined *adivasi* development strategy.

The following table shows the funds allocated for the tribal development under the Five-Year Plans in the country.

Table 1: The Allocation of Funds for Tribal Development under the Five Year Plans

Sr. No.	*Plans*	*Amount*
1.	1st Five Year Plan (1951-56)	25 Crore
2.	2nd Five Year Plan (1956-61)	50 Crore
3.	3rd Five Year Plan (1961-66)	59.39 Crore
4.	4th Five Year Plan (1970-74)	84.20 Crore
5.	5th Five Year Plan (1975-79) TSP	119.31 Crore*
6.	6th Five Year Plan (1980-85) TSP	486.11 Crore*
7.	7th Five Year Plan (1986-90) TSP	846.95 Crore*
8.	8th Five Year Plan (1991-95) TSP	1484.12 Crore*
9.	9th Five Year Plan (1997-2001) TSP	2009.61 Crore*
10.	10th Five Year Plan (2002-07) TSP	2136.39 Crore*

Source: An Overview of Tribal Research Studies by Jain and Tribhuwan, Tribal Research and Training Institute, Pune, 1995, p. 21.
* *Source*: Government of India: Ministry of Tribal Affairs, *Annual Report 2005-2006*, New Delhi, p. 61.

The Government of India, in 1972, evolved the Tribal Sub-Plan strategy using inputs from the Expert Committee under the Chairmanship of Professor S.C. Dube. The Expert Committee was set up by the Ministry of Education and Social Welfare. By the end of the Fourth Five Year Plan, the number of Tribal Development Blocks in the country rose to 504. (However, this strategy failed to address the development of *adivasi* populations that dwelt outside these blocks.

The Tribal Sub-Plan strategy was adopted for the first time in the Fifth Five Year Plan and this practice continued in all subsequent plans. It could be said that the actual development of *adivasis* was initiated from the Fifth Five Year Plan through the concept of the Tribal Sub-Plan for the tribal regions. The objectives of the Tribal Sub-Plan (TSP) were twofold, and included socio-economic development of Scheduled Tribes along with their protection against exploitation.

The TSP strategy adopted since the Fifth Five Year Plan resulted in a manifold increase in the flow of funds to TSP from about Rs. 1,000 crore during the Fifth Five Year Plan to Rs. 10,000 crore during the Seventh Five Year Plan. Benefits of such incremental investment have not, however, reached the tribals in equal measure.[8]

In order to ensure effective implementation of the Tribal Sub-Plan, 191 Integrated Tribal Development projects, 277 pockets of tribal concentration known as Modified Area Development Approach projects, 73 micro projects for primitive tribal groups, and 32 clusters were established in the country. Moreover, the development of Scheduled Tribes was given recognition in the 20-Point Programme, 1986.

However, the vicious circle of problems pertaining to *adivasis* continued and included the fundamental need to livelihood, food security, health, education, rights over natural resources, and inhuman practices like bonded labour.

To deal with the problem of bonded labour, the Government of India had already enacted the Bonded Labour System (Abolition) Act in 1976. Under this Act, the identification and rehabilitation of bonded labourers is the responsibility of the concerned state government. Nevertheless, the existence of the bonded labour system in one form or other was reported from 11 states, namely, Andhra Pradesh, Bihar, Gujarat, Rajasthan, Karnataka, Kerala, Madhya Pradesh, Maharashtra, Orissa, Tamil Nadu, and Uttar Pradesh. The Gandhi Peace Foundation's survey estimated the number of bonded labourers to be 26.17 lakh. The National Sample Survey Organisation had conducted a survey of bonded labour along with their 32nd Round in 1977-78. According to this survey, the number of bonded labourers was 3.25 lakh.[9] A majority of the bonded labourers belonged to the Scheduled Tribes and were engaged in mines, quarries, brick kilns, and farming activities.

The existing issue-based policies employed contradict the macro-level policies and so the objective of holistic development of the *adivasi*s still eludes us and has not been achieved even after 65 years of democratic governance. In spite of the protection given to the tribal population by the Constitution of India, tribals still remain the most backward ethnic group in India. They rate very low on three of the most important indicators of development: health, education, and income.[10]

I.2 *Adivasis* in Maharashtra

The *adivasi* population in Maharashtra according to the 2011 Census was 1,05,10,213 (9.37 per cent). *Adivasis* are predominantly rural and live mostly in the forest and hilly areas spread over in 47 tehsils of 15 districts. The *adivasi* population in the scheduled areas is about 37.67 lakh, i.e. (52 per cent) of the total tribal population of the state. The scheduled areas notified by the Government of India consist of 5,809 villages and 12 towns in 15 districts covering an area of 46,531 sq. km, which is about 15.1% of the area of the state. These districts are Thane, Pune, Nashik, Dhule, Nandurbar, Jalgaon, Ahmednagar, Nanded, Amaravati, Yeotmal, Gadchiroli, Raigarh, Bhandara, Gondia and Chandrapur. The Tribal Sub-Plan (TSP) area covers the scheduled area. In addition, the state government felt that 773 villages in the districts of Raigarh, Bhandara, Gondia, Chandrapur, Yeotmal and Pune reserved to be extended for the benefits of TSP, though these villages did not strictly satisfy the criteria laid down by the Government of India for inclusion in the TSP area.[11]

As in the case of India, development of *adivasi*s in Maharashtra state is undertaken through the Tribal Sub Plan since the beginning of the Fifth Five Year Plan. The TSP is mainly an area development plan. Scheduled areas of heavy tribal concentration were formed into special development blocks. However, it was revealed after 10 years of implementation of the TSP that this did not result in improvement of living conditions of the tribals and benefits had not percolated downwards.[12] Therefore, the Government of Maharashtra appointed a committee in 1987 to examine and recommend new guidelines. The committee submitted its report and the

Government of Maharashtra issued modified orders in the matter vide resolution dated September 21, 1992.

In the year 2006, the Sukhthankar Committee suggested that the government should make a provision of budget on the basis of the total *adivasi* population so as to develop the status of *adivasis* through the Tribal Sub-Plan. However, a provision of only 4.85% of the budget was made for the year 2005-06.[13] This shows that the government was unwilling to make appropriate provisions for marginalised groups. The failure of the government has resulted in more marginalisation of *adivasis*, for example, 67% tribes and 91.08% primitive tribes were below the poverty line in Maharashtra.[14] The proportion of child death and malnutrition was very high among the *adivasis*, i.e. about 15% *adivasi* children were malnourished. It was stated in the report of the Government of Maharashtra, 2005, that every year, malnutrition caused about 2 lakh child deaths.[15]

Thus, the data shows that the state failed to achieve human development through its policies and programmes. Why did this happen? It is important to understand the development approach followed by the state and the implications of this approach, and given the focus of this study, the implications specifically on *adivasis*. For identifying the reasons for failure of the government programmes of development in general and programmes meant for *adivasis* in particular, it is necessary to have a quick look at government strategies and perspectives of development. Failures of the government in making pro-people policies stem from lack of people's participation in programme designing and implementation.

I.3 The Role of the State Agency for Development

As enshrined in the Constitution, the government maintained its agenda of social justice through the implementation of development programmes. Several schemes/programmes were evolved for the development of weaker sections. The Community Development Programme (CDP), 1952, covered development of agriculture-related matters, irrigation, communication, education, health, supplementary employment, housing, social welfare, and training for agricultural activities. The programmes continued with the objective of reaching the last person. They aimed to raise the status and included the Minimum Needs Programme, Special Programme for Small Farmers and Agricultural Labourers, Rural Industries Projects and Rural Artisans Programmes, the Antyodaya Programme, Rural Works Programme, Crash Scheme for Rural Development, Pilot Intensive Rural Employment Scheme, Special Employment Scheme, Food for Work Programme, National Rural Employment Programme and Tribal Development Agencies, and the Tribal Sub-Plan. Significantly, there were special interventions for the alleviation of rural poverty, which focused on the Integrated Rural Development Programme (IRDP), High Yielding Varieties, and Green Revolution. Sociologists and anthropologists reviewed these programmes and observed that the programmes became excessively bureaucratised and development-centred around the upper strata. Whether it is in the matter of wage/loan payment or delivering goods/services, or supervision over works, it is the officials/bureaucrats who deal with the various aspects of implementation. Officials have been assigned roles in implementation since the beginning of the First Five Year Plan. At the same time, corruption plagued the implementation of many such programmes.[16]

As we know, a majority of *adivasi* communities across the country are dependent on forests for their livelihoods. However, the relation between *adivasis* and the forest department has been one of conflict and confrontation wherein forest-dependent communities have been labelled as '*encroachers*'. This resulted in alienation and exclusion of *adivasis* from their historical rights over natural resources.

With the adoption of the new economic policy, lands were taken away by the states for different projects. After 1990, it was the private industries and enterprises that took hold of the tribal lands. The economic policy of liberalisation, globalisation, and privatisation also affects the community sector, as such policies work towards relaxing the protective provisions made for the betterment of indigenous communities all over the country. The government lacks the political will to check this and the process of *adivasi* land alienation has accelerated.

In the name of 'national interest', construction activities, large dams, mega industrial and mining projects were carried out in the post-reform period, i.e. 1991 onwards. This alienation was accelerated using the euphemism "privatisation of natural resources". Although in recent years, a number of legislations have been enacted to preserve the rights of the tribal community over land, landlessness among them has considerably increased.

Discrimination in the labour market is another important factor contributing to increased poverty among *adivasis*. Compared to other social groups, a substantially higher proportion of the Scheduled Tribe population is involved in manual employment such as agricultural and construction activities. The level of occupational diversification is also very low. In the year 2004 more than 70% of them were dependent on agriculture either as self-employed or casual labourers.[17] With the onslaught of liberalisation, privatisation, and globalisation, the *adivasis* have been subjected to massive exploitation and repression.[18] For instance, in Kalinganagar in Odisha, on January 2, 2006, 12 *adivasis* were killed by the police when they protested against forceful 'taking over of their land' by the Government of Odisha to set up steel units for the private companies. It has also been observed that these communities could not become a part of development processes but have instead become marginalised through the process of 'development-induced displacement'.

The Planning Commission's estimates of poverty, based mainly on consumption flows, indicate that the proportion of persons below the poverty line among Scheduled Tribes is substantially higher than the national average. In 1993-94, the percentage of the Scheduled Tribe population living below the poverty line in rural areas was 51.92 and that in urban areas was 41.14, whereas the overall percentages were 37.27 and 32.36, respectively.[19] The figures for 1993-94 provide an illustration of this, which is significant even though lower than the nearly 20% level of 1983-84.

If we see the government reports on estimation of poverty in India in 1993-94, the proportion of population below the poverty line stood at around 37% and this was brought down to 27% by 1999-2000. However, at the same time, the calorie intake information for the year 1993-94 collected by NSSO showed that nearly 70% of the rural population was in the poverty bracket.[20] Therefore, what credence does one give to the official estimation poverty line of 27% for the year 1999-2000? Moreover frequent starvation deaths, especially in *adivasi* belts, on one hand, and increasing agriculture labourers' migration to cities on the other, indicate a crisis in rural areas.

Reduction in poverty among the *adivasi*s was also observed to be slower than for other groups. It is noteworthy that *adivasi*s in the states of Madhya Pradesh, Odisha, Bihar, and Maharashtra experienced the worst form of poverty. *Adivasi*s were seen to be caught in hard-core poverty and marginalisation in terms of land alienation which is one of the most important forms of alienation, and which takes place in various ways. Thus, large development projects including dams and mines encroached upon large tracts of forest areas, and displaced several thousand forest dwelling communities, who are still struggling to survive in the absence of human-centred rehabilitation efforts.[21] Similar displacement has been caused by large industrial development projects and increasing urbanisation as well. A study conducted by the Department of Rural Development shows that, of the total land from which people were displaced, about 40% was by way of sale, 25% by way of land acquisition for public purposes, 25% by way of mortgage, lease, and the remaining 10% by other modes. Through modes other than land acquisition, 80% of this land went to non-*adivasis*. [22] *Adivasi*s lost more than a million hectares of land for the construction of dams, hydroelectricity, mining, and other projects. A preliminary estimate states that from 1951 to 1985 about 14.5 million persons have been displaced due to the mines, dams, industries and wildlife sanctuaries.[23]

As compared to other sections of Indian society, the *adivasi* population has the lowest Human Development Index (HDI). In addition, *adivasis* suffer from geographical and cultural exclusion, both of which are not captured in the HDI. Similarly, lack of empowerment to make choices for themselves is also not accounted for. A large segment of the *adivasi* population lives below the poverty line and suffers from a high infant mortality rate, severe malnutrition, various communicable diseases, lower literacy rates, and an extremely slow pace of development. Underdevelopment coupled with lack of access to proper administrative and judicial machinery in *adivasi* areas further increases their deprivation.[24]

The above mentioned data reveal that the state, as a responsible agency, failed to take care of citizens and carry out proper implementation of development programmes. The reasons for the failure of tribal development programmes were at the overall policy level, at implementation level, and also due to lack of people's participation the idea of alternative development models emerged as a consequence of this failure.

Approaches to Reform

Reforms may be viewed in terms of approaches used. Such approaches evolve over time. Thus, while initially approaches such as charity and welfare are used, these are later replaced by approaches such as integrated development, social justice, and finally the most recent paradigm of the **rights-based approach that embodies empowerment of the people and their active participation.** A rights-based approach to development is a conceptual framework for human development that is normatively based on international human rights standards and operationally directed to promoting and protecting human rights. The International Development Strategy of October 1970 called for a global strategy. Another UN resolution called for a unified approach to development and planning to fully integrate social and economic aspects. 'Social equity', 'human potential', 'all sections of the population', 'structural change', were its keywords. It called for cross-sectoral integration and 'participatory development'.

The empowerment approach aims at increasing the capacities and decision-making power of the marginalised. The emphasis is on women and the rural poor as they tend to be most oppressed owing to their absence in decision-making bodies.

Ideas/notions of social development and empowerment are located in the dynamics of the legitimate sharing, distribution, and redistribution of power. During the 1980s and 90s, empowerment as a strategy was placed in the spectrum of state-sponsored development processes.

Historical evidence suggests that empowerment is possible only through sustained grassroots mobilisation, social movement, selfless interventions of civil societies (i.e. NGOs, people's cooperatives, and progressive institutions) and well-articulated alternative policy formulations along with their execution with a political commitment for the redress of power imbalances at the grassroots. Owing to this, in the contemporary development paradigm, voluntary actions initiated by NGOs occupy a significant place.

I.4 The Right to Development Approach

To put forth the rights of the people assertively, it is important to create a force, which would pressurise the state to recognise the demand. This involves a number of efforts at organising and mobilising people on the issues of rights.

Article 1 of the Declaration of the Right to Development stresses that by virtue of their inalienable right to development, every human being is entitled to participate in and contribute to development. It states that development policies can be legitimate only if they are predicated on the active, free, and meaningful participation of the people. Participation is considered as a right of the people and is not an optional gift to be bestowed to citizens by governments. In a human rights-based approach to development, participation is linked with control.

The idea of participation embodied in the human rights approach envisages people's control of planning, process, outcome, and evaluation. This perspective respects the fundamental human rights tenet that people are the subjects and the active players, who determine and freely pursue their economic, social, and cultural development. The rights-based approach is based on principles of equity, non-discrimination, participation, accountability, and transparency.[25]

The right to development puts the responsibility for ensuring development on everyone—-individuals, national governments, and the international community. All human beings have a responsibility for development, both individually and collectively, states Article 4 of the Declaration. States have the responsibility to create national and international conditions favourable for the realisation of the right. Borrowing from the ideas of Amartya Sen and Mahbub ul-Huq, UNDP launched the idea of human development, which embraces human needs as social goals beyond material well-being such as higher standards of education and health, wider opportunities for work and leisure, increased capabilities and choices for an individual. As argued by Amartya Sen, development can be seen as 'a process of expanding the real freedoms that people enjoy'.[26]

The constructive part of development is reflected when people can positively achieve economic opportunities, political liberties, social power, enabling conditions of good health, transparency, guarantees, protective security, economic facilities, and entitlement of basic rights, basic education, encouragement, and initiatives. Development can also be seen, as the recognition of entitlement in itself, as an act of empowerment. Recognising the fact that each and everyone is entitled to rights, constitutes the crucial step towards self-development. The ability of the poor and marginalised to break the evils of oppressive fear and injustice is the key to their access to any process of socio-political and economic development. This process of empowerment requires a rights-based perspective and the facilitating role of organisations and institutions to create an enabling environment for people to realise their own potential to change their lives. Change in the lives of the marginalised people happens when they are able to assert their rights and make creative interventions against unjust and unequal power relationships in society.

Control over natural resources is a very crucial and vital component of participation. The entitlement over natural resources for livelihood and enhancing quality of life often determines the agrarian structure and power relations. However, fair distribution of land, water, and forest resources has remained rhetoric despite various laws and commissions.

The aggregate expenditure by states on the social sector came down from 35.39% in 1991-92 to 33.96% in 2000-01, i.e. from 5.82% to 5.77% of GDP.[27] Thus, the government's annual budget for the social sector was inadequate. Even when the allotted budget is adequate, it may not result in improving the quality of services as has been the case with educational services.

Rural development has failed at various levels. Thus the government was unable to create local institutions that serve the needs of the poor or create sustainable, active, and responsive grassroots organisations owing both to the lack of political will as well as the use of top-down models of rural development.[28]

Failures of the Indian state resulted in the sudden increase of alternative development initiatives by Voluntary Organisations after the Emergency. The emergence of Voluntary Organisations is not just due to the failure of the government but also that of organised political parties, trade unions, and other traditional forms of opposition to the ruling elite. Our mixed economy is composed of large state and corporate sectors. Both failed in creating opportunities for the people.[29] This crisis situation motivated youth all over the country to initiate people's movements and grassroots social action groups—the phenomenon of non-party political formations. The failure of the development strategy of the Indian state led to the rise of small action groups as agencies of people's initiatives in favour of the alienated and the oppressed sections of society. There was a growing political self-awareness among the *adivasis* of India as they began a struggle to reclaim their rights over the natural resources and human dignity, habitat and political space. Struggle for survival and dignity is crucial even more so at a time when the state is trying to mortgage or sell natural resources like forests, land, water and minerals to big corporations, private developers and international financial agencies. An account of the failure of the state in dealing with the social sector, particularly in the post-reform period was presented.

Initiatives of Voluntary Organisations engaged in welfare activities have a long history in India. In the last four decades, their initiatives appear to be noteworthy and some have demonstrated positive results. The following section, therefore, is devoted to a brief account of volunteerism.

A review of literature follows so as to develop the scope of the study. The review largely focuses on the marginalised and the role of Voluntary Organisations and their initiatives for grassroots development. The following section deals with some selected studies on Voluntary Organisations.

II. LITERATURE REVIEW ON THE ROLE OF VOLUNTARY ORGANISATIONS: AN OVERVIEW

The role of the state in development has been assumed to be welfare-oriented. The state has to take care of its citizens with special efforts for the oppressed and marginalised people. Owing to the failure of the state machinery in its performance, the government failed in attaining its considerable welfare goals. The government did not fulfil its promises stated in its policies and programmes. The failure is revealed in government reports, especially through the indicators such as health, education, agriculture, food security, and the supply of various civic amenities. On account of the state failures, alternative development organisations, Non-Governmental Organisations and people's organisations arose for the development of marginalised sections.

Voluntary action is a three-stage process. First, it is based on social conscience. Second, social action emerges from social consciousness generated by organised groups of people who are committed to a people-centred approach. Third, organisations of various target groups, particularly from among the weaker sections, emerge.[30] Having a big voluntary sector in our country, we need to understand the role of Voluntary Organisations, especially in the interests of the marginalised sections of society. Numerous studies have been carried out on Voluntary Organisations, working for the development of weaker sections of society including Scheduled Castes, Scheduled Tribes, and women. Here is an attempt to review some of these studies. Since the focus of the present study is on conscientisation and empowerment of *adivasis'* participation in the decision-making process by the interventions of people's organisations, the following review focuses on the social aspects such as social development, empowerment, and conscientisation of the oppressed sections.

Shareen Banu (2003) examined the role of two NGOs in Karnataka, viz. Mahila Samkhaya and Institute of Social Studies Trust, engaged in political education, training and support for the women representatives in Panchayat Raj institutions. The former was engaged in training women belonging to the Scheduled Caste category and the latter had programmes of training-cum-awareness generation for elected women representatives of all categories. Her study based on secondary sources, i.e. project reports, concludes that the training helped women representatives to gain confidence in actively participating in Gram Panchayat meetings and made women representatives capable of overcoming the structural domination.[31]

Raj Kumar (2002) studied the role of NGOs in capacity building of Panchayats for rural development in the states of Haryana, Madhya Pradesh, and Uttar Pradesh. The author covered three civil society organisations, namely, Society for Participatory Research in Asia (PRIA), Association of Voluntary Associations for Rural Development (AVARD), and Mazdoor Kisan Shakti Sangathan (MKSS) working among the Scheduled Castes, Scheduled Tribes, and women, especially with the Panchayat members.[32]

Ashish Bhatt (2004) studied a variety of Voluntary Organisations working in the remote tribal areas of Madhya Pradesh.[33] Economic upliftment and awareness for education are the two major areas where the impact of their work is seen most. The other areas are enhancement in the spirit of unity, improvement in technical knowledge, improved awareness about health, check on migration, improved saving habits through Self-Help Groups (SHGs), and women's empowerment.

B.G. Tilak Jandhyala's study on the *Role of NGOs in Education in India* (2004) highlighted the significance of Voluntary Organisations in the field of education for the neglected communities and elimination of child labour in the states of Andhra Pradesh, Madhya Pradesh, and Rajasthan. The author studied a few educational organisations, namely: M. Venkatarangayya Foundation (Hyderabad), which focuses on elimination of child labour and putting children back in schools; Kishor Bharati, a voluntary organisation in Madhya Pradesh that launched a special programme for dropouts; Ekalavya, an organisation that developed teaching-learning material for the primary schools; and Tilonia (Rajasthan) introduced an innovative educational programmes meant for street children and working children.[34] The study examined the role of NGOs in improving the standard of education in India through significant demonstration effects, to influence public action and policies of the government and also of other NGOs.

D.C. Sah (2004) studied the role of two civil society organisations in the context of natural resources and livelihood rights of tribals in southwestern Madhya Pradesh.[35] His paper on 'Partnership Ethics and Environmental Politics' argues that after independence, the new paradigm of development fundamentally altered three crucial bases of the tribal production: water, land, and forest. The community management of natural resources has been done by two crucial civil society institutions like the Adivasi Mukti Sanghtana and the Narmada Bachao Andolan. These organisations mobilised the *adivasis* of the region against repressive acts of the state and the market. In remote rural areas, market and state failure have motivated intense community participation in informal institutions that govern land-man relations, and law and dispute resolution.

Rahul Ramagundam (2001) studied the Ekta Parishad Movement, the well-known struggle for the rights of *adivasis* in Madhya Pradesh.[36] This study was based on the land rights campaign for the *adivasis* in Murena, Chambal, Bundelkhand, Baghelkhand, and Mahakushal regions of Madhya Pradesh and in Chhattisgarh. The study highlighted the organising and mobilising strategies for the assertion of rights of *adivasis*. In Madhya Pradesh, Ekta Parishad has been in the forefront in bringing awareness and consequent empowerment of the *adivasis* by effecting their organisations at the village level. Since 1990, the Parishad has been working for the *adivasis'* rights, especially control over natural livelihood resources such as forest, land, and water. Ekta Parishad organised the six month Bhu-Adhikar Padyatra (Land Rights long-march) on December 10, 1999 to June 20, 2000. Ekta Parishad's National Convenor P.V. Rajgopal launched the land rights campaign to bring the issues of landlessness to the forefront of policy makers. Success of the *Padyatra* resulted in the cultivation of grassroots activists, leadership of *adivasis*, identification of *adivasis'* land, and benefits to the land alienated families.

Anil Bhatt's study *Development and Social Justice* (1989) was based on the Gujarat experience of grassroots groups. These grassroots organisations attempt to redefine politics as something different and beyond electoral and legislatives politics, i.e. health, rights over community resources, ecological and cultural issues. The author studied more than thirty social action groups, which were primarily working on the issues of economic, educational, social justice, social reform, and conscientisation activities.[37] This study highlights the impact of grassroots initiatives which resulted in considerable increase in agriculture production and prevention of exploitation by the capitalists. Owing to the activities of the organisations such as educational, social awareness, and social action they were able to achieve more than before. By organising social awareness *shibirs* (camps), they have had considerable impact in bringing about a sense of brotherhood and unity among *adivasi*s.

Daniel Crowell (2003) studied the Self-Employed Women's Association (SEWA) in Banaskantha and Kutch districts of Gujarat.[38] SEWA's development programmes were carried out mainly in rural areas through organising and mobilising people in villages. SEWA's broad strategy was to build the capacity of vulnerable people and provide them with need-based programmes and demand-driven activities. The study highlighted some crucial areas like capital formation at the household level and capacity building of its members. SEWA has invested a great deal in human development. Its proactive intervention increased employment opportunities and income; improved nutrition and access both to healthcare and childcare; enhanced housing, water and sanitation; increased assets of women; strengthened women's leadership and their self-reliance.

Satyakam Joshi (2000) studied two civil society organisations, namely, Gram Vikas Mandali and Adivasi Bhoomiheen Kisan Hakk Saurakshan Samiti working for the Dang tribals' land rights and mobilising people against the corrupt politicians.[39] These groups organised *dharnas* and *rallies* against elected representatives for implementing schemes for the poor. After the protest movement, the Government of Gujarat looked into the problem of land rights of the tribals and found that they have been cultivating the land for centuries and issued a notification for giving land titles to those who have been cultivating forest land before 1980.

John Sommer (2001) brought out an interesting study on various organisations, primarily working for the empowerment of *adivasis* and *dalits* across the country. The study throws light on the plight of bonded labourers and landless labourers, women's self-employment, organising and mobilising, lobbying with government for policy response to the needs of the poor. These are real life experiences of numerous organisations and individuals across India relating to the struggles of the oppressed.[40] This study brings out the success stories in the lives of oppressed people through the empowerment. A crucial effort of organisations has been explored in the areas of livelihood and good governance through organising, advocacy, and strengthening peoples and organisational capacities.

B. Lawani's study *NGOs in Development* (1999) focused on the role of Voluntary Organisations in the field of social welfare and social development in the Solapur district of Maharashtra state. The study reveals that more than one-third of the organisations were active in the socio-economic field. It mentions that a large number of organisations had done great work in the field of socio-cultural and charity-oriented activities. Since the socio-economic scenario has changed a lot, it is suggested that the organisations should take up new responsibilities such as social development, use of science and technology in the rural areas, human resource development. Some of the organisations brought out attitudinal changes towards eradicating social evils.[41]

An interesting paper 'Voluntary Organisations as a Catalytic Agent of Social Change' by V.V. Deshpande (2004) dealt with the watershed development in Adgaon village in Aurangabad district, Maharashtra. This study has shown that Voluntary Organisations were successful in making people proactive and hard working thus enabling them to increase food grain production.[42]

Surekha Dalvi and Milind Bokil carried out a study on *Tribal*

Communities and Land Rights in Coastal Maharashtra (2000), which focuses on the issues of *dalhi* lands (*dalhi* is the method of cultivating rice and millets on sloping lands), especially the alienation of tribal lands in Raigad and Thane District of Maharashtra. The duo studied the people's movement on *dalhi* land issues. The agitations and campaigning on the *dalhi* land issues were taken up by mass-based organisations, viz. Shoshit Jan Andolan, Bhoomi Sena, Kashtkari Sanghatana, Shramjeevi Sanghatana, Gram Swaraj Samiti, Shramik Mukti Sanghatana, Shramik Kranti Sanghatana and Sarvahara Jan Andolan. They adopted three main strategies: mass mobilisation and protest, legal means and procedural battles with the state government.[43]

The late Comrade Godavari Parulekar organised Warlis in Thane district for increase in wages and improvement in working conditions, also against the atrocities perpetrated by moneylenders and forest contractors. This created political consciousness among the Warlis.[44] Her well-known account Godavari Parulekar, *Jevha Manoos Jaga Hoto* (Marathi for when a man is awakened) (the English version of the book is titled *Adivasis Revolt*) focuses on struggles for survival of *adivasis* for their identity and dignity as human beings. She depicted her experiences through the journey of Kisan Sabha, which worked for the development of *adivasis* in Thane district of Maharashtra. These efforts helped release many bonded labourers and enabled them to fight against exploitation. The struggle was launched for conscientising the poor *adivasis* to enable them to take a position against exploitation. The struggle reflected into a strong organising of *adivasis* against moneylenders and landlords in Thane district. The spirit of exploited and suppressed people was awakened.[45]

Indra Munshi (1986) studied the socio-economic condition of the Warlis in Thane district in the 1940s. Her study dealt with the women's long struggle and release of the bonded labourers from moneylenders and landlords. She analysed forms of women's oppression in Thane district with special reference to the role of the Kisan Sabha of the Communist Party of India (CPI), which led the struggle during 1945-1947 under the leadership of both Godavari Parulekar and Shamrao Parulekar.[46] She observed that the *Warli* struggle encouraged confidence and political consciousness among the *Warli* women and men. The Kisan Sabha is a pioneering example of social action as a harbinger for development of adivasis for their rights. Indra Munshi concludes that real social development lies in creating pressure from below for becoming free from the bonded labour practice. Her study shows the implications of the work of grassroots social action for mobilising poor *adivasis* for effective implementation of legislations on the one hand, and creating alternative institutions and norms, which protect the *adivasi*s from falling into the debt trap on the other.[47]

A study of Bhoomi Sena (Land Army) was carried out by Shashi Ranjan Pandey (1991). His study focused on Community Action for Social Justice. During the late 1970s, the Bhoomi Sena was an expression of a 'spontaneous uprise' and mobilisation of the local oppressed and was founded by Shri Kaluram Dhodhade. The Bhoomi Sena continues to work for the land-entitlement of tribals, and continues to organise both farm and non-farm workers.

Vasant Deshpande (1985) focused on the struggle of the deprived for the development of *adivasi*s in Thane district. His study highlighted the struggle against the exploitation of poor *adivasi*s by moneylenders and landlords and the work of the Bhoomi Sena and the emergence of leadership within the oppressed community that refused to tolerate exploitation and injustice under the leadership provided by the young *adivasi*, Shri Kaluram Dhodhade mentioned previously and the involvement of Shri Aba Karmarkar, a dedicated urban social activist.[48] The latter organised his people and gave them the courage to stand up collectively against all types of oppression and to carry out a struggle for reclaiming the lands for the livelihood of *adivasi*s. The need to move towards development conscientisation is crucial for action under the dedicated leadership. Hence, this study revealed that grassroots action needs some support of sympathetic members of legislators and of political parties.

Another study on *adivasis* education for community development was by Rudolf Heredia (1992) in Thane district of Maharashtra.[49] He studied the impact of schools on students and the influence of schools on the tribal community in Thane district. The author tried to make a comparison between the mission, government, and other private schools. His study suggests that the initiatives and innovations are very useful for the formal and non-formal education and conscientisation for people's struggles.

Some of the above-mentioned studies focused on people's participation and conscientisation in the light of grassroots learning by doing and self-learning for the better implementation of the government's schemes. A few organisations used the human rights perspective in their work, but do not include development programmes having the rights-based approach or the twin model of development that combines organising and mobilising strategies. NGOs have emerged as a third sector, and hence it is very important to assess the response of the people and grassroots organisations engaged in conscientisation of poor *adivasis*, and their mobilisation for their rights. The following section, therefore, is devoted to a brief account of volunteerism.

III. VOLUNTEERISM IN INDIA

The term 'Voluntary Organisation' is synonymous with terms such as non-governmental organisations (NGOs), voluntary action, non-profit organisations, and grassroots social action groups. An informal and flexible structure, closeness to the communities, no limit in working hours, commitment to the people's cause, and being lively, strong and vibrant are some of the characteristics that NGOs tend to possess.

India has a unique tradition of social welfare and social work. Social work has contributed considerably to the welfare of vulnerable people. The Voluntary Organisations working for the welfare and development of the socially disadvantaged groups have already established their credentials as effective agents of social change and development by virtue of their direct contacts and linkages with target groups in implementation of various developmental programmes even in the most difficult areas where these groups reside.

The excessively centralised state failed to extend welfare benefits to the poor. Such failures of formal macro organisations as well as the failure of the top-down development approaches led to the mushrooming of grassroots organisations at the micro level. India's liberal democratic regime permissive of activism in the civil society is a fertile ground for NGOs to flourish.[50] The importance of NGOs has been increasing due to the failure of the state to deliver and the growing involvement of the enlightened and enthusiastic middle class in the NGO sector. This is evident from the professionalism displayed by NGOs in reaching out to the masses and delivering the goods, from the recognition from the state because of pressure from international declarations summits/protocols, and from the increasing faith of donor agencies in the NGOs. Since the last three decades, NGOs' effective performance has been remarkable because of their proactive involvement and commitment to the cause. NGOs have employed processes such as building awareness among masses, mobilisation of masses, mustering support from political parties, benefiting the people through their participation in various projects and programmes, and influencing the policies and programmes of the government. Another very important factor is that NGOs empower the people through their participation and by creating grassroots level popular initiatives.

In the initial phase after independence, the legacy of the Gandhian era influenced voluntary action to fulfil the unfinished tasks undertaken before independence. The efforts to further spread the Khadi and Village Industries not only became an important area of voluntary efforts but also a government responsibility. Following the death of Mahatma Gandhi in 1948, a number of freedom fighters and 'Constructive Work' followers joined Voluntary Organisations. A fellowship of brotherhood under the Sarvodaya Samaj and a coordinated organisation named Sarva Seva Sangh for all constructive work institutions were founded. Many prominent followers of Mahatma Gandhi inculcated Gandhi's spirit of voluntary efforts in the post-independence era and notables among them are Acharya Vinoba Bhave, Jayaprakash Narayan, Thakkar Bapa, and others.

Vinoba Bhave, in his attempt to transform rural India came forward with the idea of the Bhoodan and Gramdan movement in 1951 and 1952, respectively, giving a new impetus to voluntary efforts. He started the Bhoodan (Land-gift) movement in Pochampalli (Telangana in Andhra Pradesh). The essential characteristic of the movement was that the surplus lands were to be donated by landlords and redistributed to landless peasants. Similarly, his Gramdan movement started in Mangroth village in Uttar Pradesh involved community action with the ownership of land vested in the village community. Bhave further widened the concept to *Shramadan* (gift of labour), *Sampattidan* (gift of wealth), and *Buddhidan* (gift of mental abilities) for the realisation of *Sarvodaya* (welfare of all) and the benefit of society as a whole. He thus built a powerful voluntary movement, which has shown the way for peaceful transformation of rural society.

Thakkar Bapa also made a mark in the history of volunteerism in the field of education, health, and tribal development. Both Thakkar and Bhave's actions represented Gandhian ideals.

During the Third Five Year Plan, the government recognised voluntary efforts as an aspect of public cooperation and sought more cooperation from Voluntary Organisations, particularly in the rural development programmes. During the mid-1960s, many foreign NGOs entered the Indian scene to work in the voluntary sector for organising relief and rehabilitation work necessitated by severe drought and famine. These include: Foreign funds started flowing in during this period, thus changing radically the character of the voluntary sector in the country.

The National Service Scheme (NSS) formed in 1969, provided impetus to volunteerism among young students in colleges and universities, who were motivated to work on a voluntary basis for the development of weaker sections of society. The economic and political circumstances during this phase motivated new generations of people to enter the voluntary sector.

With the state emergency followed by Indira Gandhi's fall and defeat of the Congress Party, the country's political scenario changed and the Janata Party came to power in 1977. The Janata government assigned a special role to Voluntary Organisations and thus began a new phase in the history of voluntary efforts in India. The government visualised a special role for Voluntary

Organisations through its programmes such as the Adult Education, Block Level Planning and Training programmes of lower level functionaries. The industrial and business houses were granted special tax exemption to involve Voluntary Organisations in rural development work.

At that time, several unions, trade unions, community-based organisations, and many agents of development started their work in neglected areas and are representative of alternative modes of development thinking in India. The failure of the government was accepted and the initiatives of Voluntary Organisations were promoted through various plans and commissions.

From independence in 1947, until the Sixth Five Year Plan (1980-85), there were a few efforts on the part of the government to define the role of a voluntary agency or to recognise the importance of NGOs in the development planning. Realising the importance of participatory development, the Sixth Five Year Plan document emphasised the importance of non-governmental organisations, both formal and informal in nature, as new actors, which could motivate and mobilise people in specific or general developmental activities. Through the Seventh Five Year Plan, the government not only accepted the NGOs' vibrant role in development and social transformation, but also provided them a substantial funding support to the tune of about Rs. 150-200 crore.[51]

India currently has a large number of Voluntary Organisations or Non-Profit Organisations (NPOs)—about 1.2 million across the country. In the year 2007 a study of Non-Profit Institutions was undertaken by the Society for Participatory Research in Asia (PRIA), Delhi, in collaboration with the Institute of Policy Studies, Johns Hopkins University, USA. According to this study, the voluntary sector generated a sum of Rs. 17,922 crore (over Rs. 179 billion) in the year 1999-2000 through self-generated funds, government funds, and private funds. These organisations were engaged in a wide spectrum of activities cutting across the economic, social, cultural, and scientific domains. These groups involved as many as 19.2 million people, many of whom worked on a voluntary basis.[52] The survey estimated that approximately over 16 million persons were working as volunteers. This is equivalent to 2.7 million paid employees and 3.4 million full-time volunteers, a total of 6.1 million, which is considerable given the fact that the central government employees in 2000 numbered only 3.3 million.

VOs as Intermediaries Between the State and the People

The efforts made by the government for making development policies and schemes have not yielded results for the poor *adivasi*s due to their lack of active participation, awareness, and power to assert their rights. Though India has a rich tradition in voluntary services, the role of Voluntary Organisations in social transformation, social development, economic and political empowerment with a rights-based perspective is yet to be thoroughly understood even after five decades of planning. The contribution of social action groups in the last two decades has helped to build a sense of dignity and social consciousness among the marginalised communities. Consequently, the study of development initiatives by Voluntary Organisations is crucial and relevant in the current time.

A growing number of development–oriented Voluntary Organisations across the country have engaged themselves in critical areas such as the environment, livelihood, human rights, women's empowerment, and *adivasi* rights. Voluntary Organisations have an important role to play in tribal development. This has been recognised over the years and it is the accepted principle that deserving Voluntary Organisations should not only be helped but consciously built up in the field of tribal development.[53]

Voluntary agencies have, over the past few decades, made significant contributions to the well-being of neglected groups in terms of education, sensitisation, etc. Innovative programmes of many voluntary agencies have often highlighted the need for decentralised participation and local control leading to new experimentation, and re-questioning the development process.

To achieve the Tenth Five Year Plan objective of empowering disadvantaged groups, Voluntary Organisations were encouraged not only to play a key role in promoting people's initiative and participation, but also in acting as designated informants to assist both the government and the target groups to fight against social evils like untouchability, atrocities against these groups and their economic and social exploitation, and helping to ensure social justice to the marginalised groups. Therefore, the government created spaces and encouraged VOs. Thus, Voluntary Organisations were made an important bridge between grassroots and the state. They thus became instrumental in bringing about conscientisation and the spirit of enlightenment and in implementing development programmes of livelihood while raising awareness about basic rights and issues of governance, especially for marginalised communities.[54]

Voluntary agencies have, over the past few decades, made significant contributions to the well-being of neglected groups in terms of education, sensitisation, etc. Innovative programmes of many voluntary agencies have often highlighted the need for decentralised participation and local control leading to new experimentation, and re-questioning the development process.

The author has discussed failures in the implementation of welfare programmes in general and of tribal development in particular, and the contribution of voluntary agencies to ensure social justice.

IV. RATIONALE FOR THE STUDY

As discussed in previous sections, traditional approaches to development in India and elsewhere did not prove equal to the task of ensuring a just society, especially for the most socially, economically, and psychologically oppressed people. NGOs are known for their virtues of human touch, dedication, flexibility, innovation, self-reliance, closeness to the community, and commitment to the cause. The voluntary agencies, particularly at the community level are closer to the people than governmental agencies. Hence the government motivated voluntary agencies to shoulder various responsibilities. It is not just the government's response to Voluntary Organisations but the fact is that the NGOs are the ones that really care for the uncared sections and the people at the bottom of the social stratum. Their work is people-centred and hence they reach the unreached rural poor and work with them. They strive to promote the lives of the oppressed, deprived, marginalised, impoverished, downtrodden, helpless, powerless, deserted, and poverty-stricken in the rural areas.

The present *Draft National Tribal Policy* mentions the failures of the government to empower the poor *adivasis* even after 60+ years of independence. *The human development indicators of the ST population are much lower than the HDI of the rest of the population in terms of all parameters such as education, health, employment, income, etc.*[55] Therefore, the Government of India created special space for Voluntary Organisations and non-governmental organisations as catalysts and facilitators to help the benefits of government programmes and policies to reach the grassroots level. Keeping in mind the positive approach of Voluntary Organisations, NGOs are encouraged to get involved in tribal development activities, particularly in the running of residential and non-residential schools, hostels, dispensaries, hospitals, vocational training centers, awareness programmes and capacity-building.

The fundamental weakness lies in the state-controlled development programmes in which people for whom the development is intended are not involved in the planning, implementing, and monitoring of various programmes. Another major problem is a certain lack of awareness and conscientisation of neglected communities as a social dimension. Hence, civil society organisations are bridging the gap between the state and grassroots with the intervention of people-centred and rights-based advocacy, organising and mobilising abilities in them.

Voluntary Organisations have found strikingly effective and innovative ways by which people may secure their human and civil rights, and realign power relations in society. The question therefore is: how have VOs enabled the poor, illiterate, and marginalised to pursue their own interests and their own struggles for justice and equality? To what extent has voluntary action affected relations of the marginalised with upper caste, dominant-dependent relations? This needs to be studied. It is, therefore, planned to carry out a study on the role of non-government initiatives with special reference to Vidhayak Sansad and Shramjeevi Sanghatana in Thane district of Maharashtra state.

NOTES

1. In this study the term *adivasi* is used interchangeably with scheduled tribe.
2. Sen, Amartya: *Development As Freedom*, Oxford University Press, New Delhi, 1999, p. 4.
3. Government of India: Ministry of Tribal Affairs, Report of the High Level Committee on Socio-Economic, Health and Educational Status of the Tribal Communities of India, May 2014, New Delhi, p. 34.
4. Government of India: Ministry of Tribal Affairs, *Scheduled Tribes and Scheduled Areas, Annual Report 2003-2004*, New Delhi, 2003-04, p. 28.
5. Shah, Ghanshyam: *Social Movements in India, Tribal Movements*, Sage Publications, New Delhi, 2005, p. 92.
6. Jain, Navinchandra and Tribhuwan, Robin: *An Overview of Tribal Research Studies, Demographic Profile of Tribals in India with Special Reference to Maharashtra*, Tribal Research and Training Institute, Government of Maharashtra, Pune, 1995, p. 3.
7. Government of India, Ministry of Tribal Affairs: *Report of the High Level Committee on Socio-Economic, Health and Educational Status of Tribal Communities of India*, May 2014, p. 53.
8. Government of India, Ministry of Welfare: *Report of the Working Group on Development and Welfare of Scheduled Tribes during the Eighth Five Year Plan*, 1990-95, New Delhi, November, 1989, p. 1.
9. Ibid., p. 37.
10. Sinha, Archana: Economic Empowerment and Amelioration of Tribals in India, *Kurukshetra*, July 2006, Vol. 54, No. 9, pp. 3-11.
11. http/:www.census2011.co.in/district/355-thane.html.
12. Government of Maharashtra: *Development of Tribals*, Tribal Development Department, Government Press, Mumbai, 1992.
13. Samarthan: *Budget Maharashtra State 2006-07*, Centre for Budget Studies, Mumbai, 2006, p. 15.
14. Government of Maharashtra: *Adivasi Vikas Parichay*, Commission for Tribal Development, Government Press, Mumbai, 2003-04, p. 9.
15. Government of Maharashtra: *Child Death Evaluation Committee, Second & Final Report*, Family Welfare Department, Pune, March 24, 2005, p. 60.
16. Doshi, S.L. and Jain, P.C.: *Rural Sociology*, Rawat Publications, Jaipur, 1999, p. 274.
17. Parikh, Kirit and Radhakrishna: *India Development Report, 2004-2005*, Oxford University Press, New Delhi, 2005, p. 48.
18. Louis, Prakash: Disempowering Masses, The Scheduled Tribes, *Alternative Economic Survey of India, 2005-2006*, Danish Books,

Delhi, 2006, pp. 287-295.

19. Mander, Harsh: *Tribal Policy; Pulling Back from the Brink?* Multiplexus Press, New Delhi, 2004, p. 19.
20. *Securing Rights: Citizens Report on Millennium Development Goals*, Books for Change, Bangalore, 2005, p. 9.
21. Government of India: Ministry of Agriculture, National Commission on Farmers, *Draft National Policy for Farmers*, New Delhi, April 13, 2006, p. 21.
22. Government of India: Ministry of Welfare, *Report of the Working Group on Development and Welfare of Scheduled Tribes during the Eighth Five Year Plan, 1990-1995*, New Delhi, November, 1989, p. 35.
23. Thakur, Ashutosh: *Tribal Development and its Paradoxes*, Authors Press, New Delhi, 2001, pp. 216-217.
24. Government of India: Ministry of Tribal Affairs, *Draft National Tribal Policy*, New Delhi, July 5, 2006.
25. Centre for Development and Human Rights: *The Right to Development: A Primer*, Sage Publications, New Delhi, 2004, pp. 48-53.
26. Sen, Amartya: *Development As Freedom*, Oxford University Press, New Delhi, 1999, pp. 36-40.
27. Joshi, Seema: Impact of Economic Reforms on Social Sector Expenditure in India, *Economic and Political Weekly*, January 28, 2006, p. 361.
28. Pandey, Shashi Ranjan: *Community Action for Social Justice*, Sage Publications, New Delhi, 1991, p. 17.
29. Kothari, Rajni: The Non-Party Political Process, *Economic and Political Weekly*, February 4, 1984, p. 218.
30. Lawani, B.T.: *NGOs in Development*, Rawat Publications, Jaipur, 1999, p. 33.
31. Banu, Shareen C.P.: The Substantive Democracy; Role of Civil Society in Rural Karnataka, *Indian Anthropologist*, 2003,Vol. 33, No. 2, pp. 53-77.
32. Kumar, Raj: Capacity Building of Panchayats for Rural Development: Some Emerging Areas for NGOs, *Man & Development*, March, 2002, pp. 64-71.
33. Bhatt, Ashish: Voluntary Organisations and Tribal Development in Madhya Pradesh, in Sah, D.C. and Sisodia, Yatindra Singh, *Tribal Issues in India*, Rawat Publications, Jaipur, 2004, pp. 126-133.
34. Tilak, Jandhyala B.G.: Role of NGOs in Education in India, *Man & Development*, June, 2004, pp. 17-23.
35. Sah, D.C.: Partnership Ethics and Environmental Politics, in Sah, D.C. and Sisodia, Yatindra Singh, *Tribal Issues in India*, Rawat Publications, Jaipur, 2004, pp. 307-322.

36. Ramagundam, Rahul: *Defeated Innocence*, Grassroots India Publishers, New Delhi, 2001.
37. Bhatt, Anil: *Development and Social Justice*, Sage Publications, New Delhi, 1989.
38. Crowell, Daniel W.: *The SEWA Movement and Rural Development*, Sage Publications, New Delhi, 2003.
39. Joshi, Satyakam: State, Forest and Tribal Rights; The Case of Dangs Tribals, *Man & Development*, September, 2000, pp. 137-147.
40. Sommer, John G.: *Empowering the Oppressed*, Sage Publications, New Delhi, 2001.
41. Lawani, B.T.: *NGOs in Development*, Rawat Publications, Jaipur, 1999.
42. Deshpande, V.V.: NGOs and Development, in Pawar, S.N., et al., Rawat Publications, Jaipur, 2004.
43. Dalvi, Surekha and Bokil, Milind: In Search of Justice, Tribal Communities and Land Rights in Coastal Maharashtra, *Economic and Political Weekly*, August 5, 2000, pp. 2843-2850.
44. Kulkarni, Sharad: *Tribal Communities in Maharashtra, Struggles for Survival*, National Centre for Advocacy Studies, Pune, 2002, pp. 262-265.
45. Parulekar, Godavari: *Jevha Manoos Jaga Hoto*, Mauj Prakashan, Mumbai, 1999.
46. Saldhana, Munshi Indra: Tribal Women in the Warli Revolt 1945-47, *Economic and Political Weekly*, April 26, 1986, Vol. XXI, No. 17.
47. Saldanha, Munshi Indra: Attached Labour in Thane, *Economic and Political Weekly*, May 20, 1989, p. 1126.
48. Deshpande, Vasant: *Adivasis of Thane*, Dastane Publications, Pune, 1985.
49. Heredia, Rudolf: *Tribal Education for Community Development, A Study of Schooling in the Talasari Mission Area*, Concept Publishing Company, New Delhi, 1992.
50. Panda, Biswambhar and Pattanaik, Binay Kumar: Effectiveness of Grassroots NGOs, *Man & Development*, June 2005, pp. 39-45.
51. Pawar, S.N., Ambekar, J.B. and Shrikant, D.: *NGOs and Development*, Rawat Publications, Jaipur, 2004.
52. Srivastava, S.S. and Tandon, Rajesh: How Large is India's Non-Profit Sector? *Economic and Political Weekly*, May 7, 2005, pp. 1948-1951.
53. Government of India, Ministry of Welfare: *Report of the Working Group on Development and Welfare of Scheduled Tribes during the Eighth Five Year Plan, 1990-95*, New Delhi, November, 1989. p. 76.
54. Government of India: *Tenth Five Year Plan*, New Delhi, 2002-07.
55. Government of India, Ministry of Tribal Affairs: *Draft National Tribal Policy*, New Delhi, July 5, 2006, p. 10.

2

Research Methodology

1. Introduction

The preceding chapter discussed the role of NGOs in development and a review of literature on Voluntary Organisations was presented. This chapter outlines the research design of the study, the objectives, hypotheses, theoretical framework, and provides a Glossary of terms.

The main thrust of the study is to examine the role of Voluntary Organisations in making people aware and assertive about their right to development. This is accomplished with clear objectives, strategies, participation, capacity-building programmes, and innovative experiments to make governance transparent and accountable.

As discussed in Chapter 1, the role of Voluntary Organisations in giving direction to grassroots politics, influencing policy makers, and advocating rights of the marginalised insignificant. India was declared a 'Welfare State' soon after attaining independence and a number of provisions were made for social welfare, under which grant-in-aid facilities were made available to the Voluntary Organisations in recognition of their services. The Government of India: Ministry of Tribal Affairs Report, 2006, says *that the task of the development of Scheduled Tribes cannot be achieved by government efforts only, the role of Voluntary Organisations or non-governmental organisations with their local roots and sense of service becomes increasingly significant.*[1] To promote voluntary action, the government allocated funds for Voluntary Organisations through various Five Year Plans.

NGOs in India are required to register with the government under the Societies Act, the Public Trust Act, the Foreign Contribution Regulation Act (1976), or under the Trade Union Act. The largest number of Voluntary Organisations registered with the Ministry of Home Affairs, Government of India was 12 lakh in the year 2007. More than 35,000 organisations were registered under the Foreign Contribution Regulation Act (FCRA), 1976. In India, there were 35,000 NGOs and social organisations receiving Rs. 7,000 crore annually.[2] Since then, there has been a substantial increase in the number of NGOs due to rising awareness and social concern, widespread poverty and deprivation, weakening of the government delivery system, and increased funding.[3]

Keeping in view the type of activities they carry out, NGOs may be classified into groups such as Charity NGOs, Relief and Rehabilitation Organisations, Service Providing Organisations, Socio-Economic Development Organisations, Empowerment, Network, Support, or Mixed-role Organisations. Another classification of Voluntary Organisations is based on different strategies and approaches. Thus,

- Under the welfare approach, facilities for education, health, drinking water, roads, communications, etc are provided to the needy. The welfare approach works during natural disasters such as floods, droughts, earthquakes, ravages of water, etc.
- The service approach includes building up infrastructure in mostly backward areas.
- The approach of development focuses on conscience raising, organising and getting social justice.
- The approach considered to be the most effective is the rights-based approach to development, which puts emphasis on human rights.

This study deals with the multiple approaches of the development organisations in the geographical area where this study was undertaken.

Due to the failure of the state to deliver, various agencies began to give support to development organisations, especially those working for the empowerment of *adivasis*. During the Emergency, workers' unions, trade unions, people's organisations, community-based organisations, and many development organisations started their work in neglected areas, including Thane. An attempt has been made to study the role of non-government initiatives with reference to the Vidhayak Sansad and Shramjeevi Sanghatana (Thane, Maharashtra) which typify grassroots people's organisations.

Map 2.1: Map of Maharashtra in India

Source: www.mapsofindia.com

Map 2.2: Map of Maharashtra with Thane District

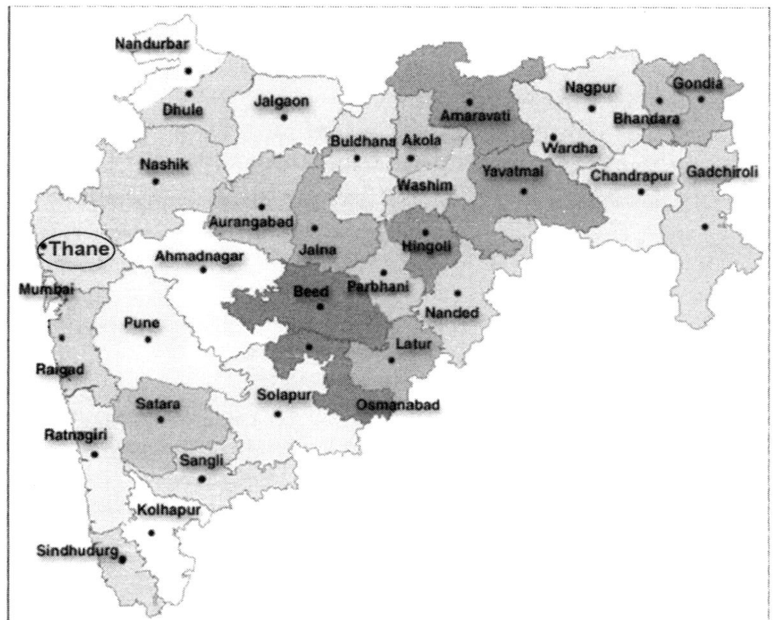

2. Universe of the Study: Thane District

The rationale for making Thane district the universe of the study was that the characteristics of the district are dire poverty, malnutrition, superstition, unemployment, lack of adequate communication, and rampant migration as well as exploitation by landlords and moneylenders.

Both the organisations have been operating in Thane district for more than three decades and were involved in various activities for the development of the underprivileged sections.

Thane is known for rich natural resources such as land, water, and forests. It is close to the metropolitan city Mumbai, the capital of Maharashtra. It is the lifeline of Mumbai in terms of supply of raw material, minerals such as sand, rock, water, bricks, fodder, and timber. However, the natural resources are exploited and the livelihood of *adivasis* is in trouble due to the increasing mega industrial plants. This leads to an adverse impact on poor *adivasis*. This makes *adivasis* more vulnerable. Thane district has a long history of social work and many organisations carried out development work in the remote areas for the *adivasis* since pre-independence times. The question that needs to be addressed is: "What were the development initiatives they undertook to improve lives of the poor?" The author, therefore, selected the district to study the impact of conscientising and mobilising efforts by these organisations.

Demographic Profile of Thane District

According to the Census, 2011, Maharashtra's total population was 11,23,74,333 whereas the schedule tribe population was 1,05,10,213, while rural population was 90,06,077 and urban were 15,04,136. The schedule tribe male population was 53,15,025 and female was 51,95,188 as per the census 2011. The state's ST population percentage is 9.4 to the total population, while 14.6 per cent was rural and just 3 per cent was urban population of the state.[4]

Thane district ranks second in the state in respect of its population of 1,10,60,148 of which male and female were 58,65,078 and 51,95,070 respectively. The rate of increase of population during the decade 1991-2001 was 54.92%. Thane district population constituted 9.84 per cent of Maharashtra's total population. The percentage of urban population in the district is 72.58% and that of rural population 27.42% as per 2001 Census. Three tahsils, viz. Talasari, Vikramgad, and Mokhada are completely rural. Population density in terms of a number of persons per sq. km was 851. The population of *adivasis* in Thane district was more concentrated in rural areas, which, according to the 2001 Census, was 47.0%, rural and just 2.6% urban. The total *adivasis* population was 11,99,290 that is 14.7%. The female population ratio among the *adivasis* was more than for other communities such as 1,004 in rural and 942 in urban areas. The Government of Maharashtra paid attention towards the development of *adivasis* and made three zones, i.e. Jawhar, Shahapur, and Dahanu, which cover almost 11 blocks of the Thane district under the Tribal Sub-Plan programmes. It is important to note that the Vasai block is a part of the development programme where we have undertaken the study.

Geographical Profile of the Study Area

Thane District forms a part of North Konkan Region, which lies between the Sahyadri hills in the east and the Arabian Sea in the West. It has a coastal line of about 113 km. It lies between 18°42' and 20°20' North latitudes and 72°45' to 73°48' East longitudes in the eastern part of the state. Its East-West spread is maximum in the South, which is about 100 km. The North-South length is approximately 140 km. The district headquarters of Thane is about 25 km from the international airport and 35 km from the main down town of Mumbai city. The total geographical area of the district is 9,558 sq. km, which is 3.11% of the total Maharashtra area.

The district receives regular, well-distributed and heavy rainfall during the south-west monsoon season. The average annual rainfall in the district is 2,576 mm. The rainfall increases from the coast towards the interior and in the coastal region decreases from the south towards the north.

Thane district is north of Mumbai along the coast of the Arabian Sea for 113 kilometres. It is divided into three topographical zones: (a) the central portion of the Sahayadri ranges and their slopes, which is mainly a forest area; (b) the eastern part, mainly paddy fields; and (c) the western plains along the coast where rice, horticulture, fodder and vegetables are grown. The documentary evidences available reveal that 'Thane' was formally known and named as 'Shreesthanak'.[5] In ancient times, Thane was an excellent port and commercial centre. From pre-historic times, Thane coast had relations with Egypt, Phoenicia, Babylon, Greece, and Persia.

Thane district was formed from the North Konkan district till 1817 and served as the district headquarters from ancient times. Its boundaries have undergone numerous changes; some parts of South Konkan district were merged with North Konkan in 1830 and 1833. The expanded North Konkan district was renamed 'Thane' district in 1833. On April 16, 1853, the first railway line was opened for traffic from Bombay to Thane. The opening of this railway line is one of the most important landmarks in the economic development not only of the Bombay-Thane region but also of the outlying areas and hinterland. The British government neither encouraged nor discouraged the creation of local self-governing institutions like municipalities for which a demand was made by the local

Map 2.3: Map of Thane District

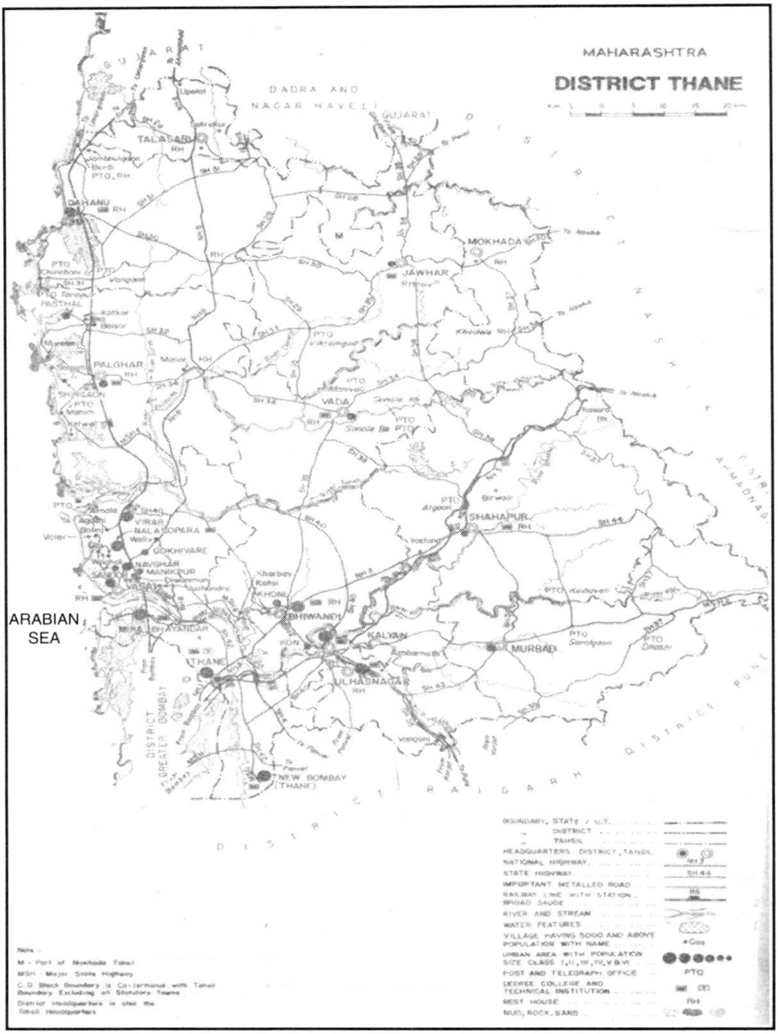

Source: Government of India, *Thane District Census Handbook*, Government Press, Mumbai, 1991.

citizens. Thane district had its first municipality at Kalyan followed by Thane and Bhiwandi.

In 1969, the tahsil of Kalyan was bifurcated into Kalyan and Ulhasnagar and since then, the district has experienced jurisdictional changes. In order to decongest Greater Bombay, the census town of New Bombay (Thane) was added in 1982 by shifting population and office complexes to New Bombay. The two new municipal corporations Thane and Kalyan were merged after 1981. Within the district, with the merger of viilages and towns in municipalities and municipal corporations, the number of villages has decreased from 1,773 in 1981 to 1,697 in 1991. The number of towns has also decreased from 34 in 1981 to 23 in 1991. At present, Thane district has 23 towns and 1,748 inhabited villages distributed among 15 tahsils, viz. Thane, Kalyan, Murbad, Bhiwandi, Shahapur, Vasai, Ulhasnagar, Ambarnath, Dahanu, Palghar, Talasari, Jawhar, Mokhada, Wada, and Vikramgad.

3. Voluntary Action in Thane District

Thane district is close to Mumbai, the capital of Maharashtra, and the economic capital of India. The district has historically suffered from state neglect which has resulted in inadequate civic amenities and overall development. With respect to population, Thane district is the second highest in Maharashtra with a population of 1,10,54,131 in 2011. In the year 2011 its *adivasi* population was 1,05,10,213.

In Thane district, voluntary action groups have been active in development activities and it is necessary to take into account the efforts of these organisations and their strategies.

In Maharashtra, in the year 2007 there were as many as 96,002 organisations, which is a substantial number and Thane district had 128 organisations registered under the Foreign Contribution Regulation Act (1976) (FCRA). The district has a history of vibrant Grassroots Organisations, Non-Governmental Organisations, People's Organisations, and Community-Based Organisations engaged in offering multiple services like charity, need-based work, service delivery, welfare, and rights-based approach to development and social change.

Volunteerism in Thane district has a long history right from pre-independence days. During 1942-45, Shamrao Parulekar worked with the Communist Party (CPM). He was jailed but released when diagnosed with TB. After being released from prison, he settled in Dahanu, a taluka place, where he witnessed tribal exploitation. During 1946-47, his wife and prominent leader, Godavari Parulekar, led the first mass movement of the *adivasi* Warlis. She opposed moneylenders and worked to emancipate bonded labourers by making poor *adivasis* as well as women aware of their rights. In Titwala, through a programme, Kisan Sabha, she mobilised *adivasis* to fight against the bonded labour system.[6] The struggle she launched was legendary and extremely effective in mobilising the masses.

In 1949, the Institute of Gokhale Education Society started its activities in Kosbad, taluka Dahanu. The agricultural institute at Kosbad initiated a variety of applied research, education, training, and direct development activities aimed at increasing the productivity of agriculture in the areas. The Institute has been conducting training courses on improved agricultural practices. Among other interventions, it helped popularise the Japanese method of cultivating paddy. The Institute also introduced wheat, gram, and vegetables as new crops to be cultivated. It also introduced new varieties of grass.

Similarly, Smt.Tarabai Modak and Anutai Wagh initiated the work of *balwadi*s for the education of Warlis in Kosbad taluka, Dahanu, in 1955 under the aegis of the Gram Bal Shiksha Kendra. This organisation conducted applied nutrition training programmes with the help of UNICEF. Gram Mangal, a well-known institute in Dahanu tahsil of Thane district, is an offshoot of the Gram Bal Shiksha Kendra. In 1957, to make tribal women self-employed, the Gram Mangal conducted a three-year programme to train them in preparation of food products, tailoring, and stationery making.

The Bhoomi Sena (Land Army) is a relatively well-known tribal organisation in Thane district. Its activities originated in Palghar taluka. It was founded by *adivasi* leader Kaluram Dhodhade, with the aim of getting back the thousands of acres belonging to the tribals that had been usurped by the *sahukars* (non-*adivasi* moneylenders). During the late 1970s, the Bhoomi

Sena received huge publicity as a "spontaneous uprise" and mobilisation of oppressed locals. It continues to work for the land-entitlement rights of tribals, and to organise both farm and non-farm workers. Its first struggle took place in village Bhatane, wherein about 600 tribals, armed with sickles, cut down the standing crop on a *sahukar's* land. Taken by surprise, the *sahukar* offered no resistance. Encouraged by this, the Bhoomi Sena continued this in 10 villages, harvesting the crop on 72 to 80 farms. The group also successfully participated in the 'Save the Forest' movement in Maharashtra and opposed the Forest Bill in 1980.

The Kashtakari Sanghatana working for Scheduled Tribes in the tehsils of Dahanu and Talasari of Thane district, emphasises rights of locals to land and forests. It provides legal aid to the oppressed and training to tribal youth. It is also involved in the right to food and right to work campaigns for better implementation of food security schemes. The Kashtkari Sanghatana succeeded in creating awareness among the tribals by evolving new teaching techniques such as performing plays that depict extreme stress and emotion. The programmes were targeted at young people to help them learn analysis and assertion, rather than just being bystanders.

The Van Mukti and the Shramik Mukti Sanghatana founded by Vijay Sathe and Indavi Tulpule operated in Thane district. These social activists paid less attention to carrying on government programmes and more to educational efforts for preparing children to assert their rights through science exhibitions, cultural festivals, and developing local leadership. In addition to assisting local development work such as water supply and afforestation, Sathe and Tulpule worked to make the government responsive by carrying out *morchas* and *dharnas* along with the *adivasis* at the Tahsildar's and Collector's offices for demands including recording of tribal huts, giving tribals their land, and providing them with employment under the landless Employment Guarantee Scheme.

The next section discusses the locale of the study village, Tilher.

Map 2.4: Map of Vasai Taluka

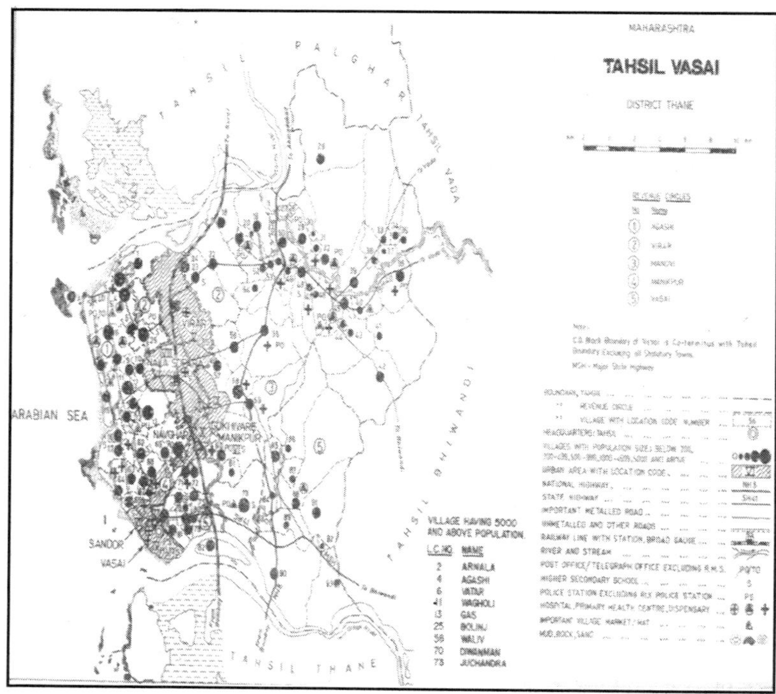

Source: Government of India, *Thane District Census Handbook*, Government Press, Mumbai, 1991.

4. Locale of the Study Village Tilher

Since 1984 both the Vidhayak Sansad and the Shramjeevi Sanghatana operate in Thane district in more than 200 villages. The village Tilher from Vasai taluka which has been selected for the study is one such village where these organisations have helped release residents from bonded labour and fought against the landlords and brick-kiln owners. The village witnesses large-scale seasonal migration to other places in search of employment. Ninety per cent of the population of the village is *adivasi.* The major *adivasi* communities are Warli, Malhar Koli, and Katkari. Most are members of Sanghatana. The focus of the study is to examine the impact of the organisations' work on the lives of *adivasis,* hence the author, has selected this village.

Tilher is situated near the Tungar hill and is located at a distance of 38 km from Vasai Taluka headquarters on the Vasai-Parol-Bhivandi route. The Tungar hill is a well known place for tourism and for the holy temple of Tungareshawar. Tilher is also close to the river Tansa. The total area of the village is 1680 hectares and the forest area is 1302 hectares. The staple food is rice. The main occupations of the villagers were the collection of non-timber wood from forest, agriculture, fishing and labour in brick-kiln industries. The village has a Group Grampanchayat and is spread along the fourteen hamlets (P*ada*), which are Tilher, Mahaskar Pada, Kuwar Pada, Khair Pada, Pali Pada, Burud Pada, Dhumal Pada, Jathav Pada, Satavi Pada, Koloshi Pada, Pared Pada, Thanekar Pada, Bij Pada, and Varatha Pada.

The village has civic amenities such as education, medical, post and telegraph, drinking water, electricity and communication. At present, the village has 6 *balwadis*, 3 *anganwadis* (Integrated Child Development Programme), and 2 primary schools. The village has well-trained medical practitioners and *pada* health volunteers. The transportation facilities and communications infrastructure are available in the village. The civic amenities such as electricity, drinking water and sanitation, health services and educational facilities are available and accessible.

The *adivasi* population comprises Warli, Malhar Koli, Mahadev Koli, Katkari, Kathodi, and M. Thakur (*Ma Thakur* as per government records). The population of the village Tilher was 3,690 according to the 2011 Census and the male-female population was 1,867 and 1,823, respectively. The total number of households was 792 and the average household size was 5.0. The total population of the Scheduled Tribes was 3,406, whereas the female population was 1,719 and the male population was 1,687. There were 1,655 literates out of 3,606 and 1,951 illiterates in the village. The Tilher has a lower literacy rate compared to Maharashtra. In 2011, the literacy rate for Tilher village was 59.81% compared to 82.34% of Maharashtra. In Tilher Male literacy stands at 70.03% while female literacy rate was 49.31%.[7] The literacy rate for males was 70.30% and for females was 49.31%. The sex ratio among *adivasis* was quite surprisingly 1,024 women per thousand men, which is far higher than the national and state sex ratios. The total workers were 2,158 and non-workers were 1,532. The land holding pattern was as usual big, small, marginal farmers and mostly cultivating rice, vegetables and pulses. The adivasis share their community characteristics with the rest of Maharashtra. They have their beliefs and superstitions, ghosts and witchcraft, fondness of songs and folk dance, laziness and carefree attitude to life. Consumption of alcohol is part of the customs as in other *adivasi* communities.

To understand the process of conscientisation among the *adivasis* in Vasai taluka, one must look at the work of both organisations in Tilher. The rationale for selecting the village was that there was rampant exploitation by outsiders and from within. Outsiders, viz. Marwaris, Parsis, Banias, and Muslims infiltrated the areas as moneylenders, shopkeepers, timber contractors, and liquor merchants. There were land grab cases registered against the landlords in the village. The *adivasis* had increasingly become victims of exploitation and had fallen into debt.

Most of the lands in the village were dry lands of extremely poor quality. Lands belonging to *adivasis* were not made fertile like non-*adivasis'* lands. There were no land levellings and no facilities of irrigation. Owing to this, the tribals had to shift their cultivation. Agricultural equipment used was generally more primitive than in other villages. *Adivasis* were socio-economically more backward than other communities.

An important feature of the area is that being just 35 km from the Mumbai-Ahmedabad highway, increasing industrialisation had resulted in land alienation. This caused disruption in the community's lifestyle and culture, which revolves around lands.

With the help of the organisations, *adivasi* families reclaimed their lands. Before the intervention of organisations, many families in the village were bonded labourers. The increasing demand for building material such as bricks, stones, sand, water and other raw material led to their extraction from the Vasai, Wada, and Bhiwandi blocks. As noted previously, *adivasis* migrated for seasonal employment and worked in brick-kilns. Many brick-kiln industries operate for the period of 6 months in a year. As brick-kiln workers, *adivasis* faced exploitation in terms of long work hours, low payments, and their children also being made to work in the brick-kilns.

Considering the socio-economic situation of the village and the history of bonded labour, the author selected this village, i.e. Tilher for the study.

The next section discusses the profile of the Voluntary Organisations selected for the study.

5. Profile of the Vidhayak Sansad and Shramjeevi Sanghatana

Brief information about other organisations working in Thane district before and after independence has been presented, but the two organisations selected for the study, viz. the Vidhayak Sansad and Shramjeevi Sanghatana stand apart from other organisations. A profile of the two organisations is presented so as to understand the development initiatives used for the rights of *adivasis* in Thane district.

While many organisations with different perspectives worked for the development of *adivasis*, many from amongst these discontinued their activities. Only a few organisations have worked for over two decades and still continue to make a difference despite changes in the socio-political scenario. Thus, the two organisations selected continue to bring about effective change by changing approaches and priorities in keeping with evolving situations. It was observed that the approach of enlightening and organising *adivasis* was very important for social change and to enhance the capacities of poor *adivasis*. These organisations also used strategies like influencing decision-makers. The dual approach of development intervention and mobilising people is based on the use of the rights-based approach, people's participation, and local leadership as instruments.

5A. Profile of the Vidhayak Sansad (A Constructive Parliament)

The anti-emergency protest included movements like *Navnirman* (reconstruction) and this was the time when several young people responded to the call for 'total revolution' by Jayaprakash Narayan. This movement was successful when the Janata Party came to power but this success was short-lived.

The founders of the Vidhayak Sansad, Vivek and Vidyullata Pandit had been members of the Rashtra Seva Dal and were active in the *Navnirman* movement, but like others, over time, they became disillusioned with party politics and decided to work for the poorest of the poor. It was with this context that the Vidhayak Sansad was formed in 1979. It was registered under the Public Trust F 5750 (Bombay) 515/79. The Pandits were inspired by various social leaders, namely, S.M. Joshi, Mahatma Gandhi, Rosa Parks, Martin Luther King, and Dr. Babasaheb Ambedkar.

Ideological Perspective of the Vidhayak Sansad

The *Vidhayak Sansad* started its work in the slums of Mumbai and in villages surrounding the city. It later evolved its goal to developing rural areas having a large proportion of socio-economically disadvantaged groups. The main aim of the Vidhayak Sansad was to bring about development of the oppressed, neglected, weaker sections, including *adivasis*, ex-untouchables, women, and other vulnerable sections of society. Residents of the villages were receptive to their work. The Pandits began with charitable welfare-oriented activities. They formed a medical centre and initiated pre-school classes, and leprosy camps in the village Dahisar. At that time, their activities were completely self-funded except for the salaries of Vivek and Vidyullata Pandit. They worked for the poor and needy with great dedication.

They later introduced cultural activities, including sports for children and youth. In the course of organising sports for the young, one day they observed that most of the young were absent and wondered about the reason for their absence. This was when they became aware about the practice of bonded labour in the area. After interacting with the tribals, they realised that the inhuman practice of bonded labour still existed. Thus began their work relating to emancipation from bonded labour for which they began organising and mobilising the *adivasis*. They also initiated activities pertaining to health and education.

After Dahisar, they extended their activities to Vasai, Wada, Shahapur, Bhiwandi, and Vikramgarh talukas of Thane district. The marginalised communities were mostly dependent on *Patil*s (headmen of villages) and were often harassed by them. There was rampant exploitation of *adivasis* from Warli, Malhar Koli, Thakar and Katkari communities by the upper castes of the society. Incidents of rape by landlords were quite common in the area. At that time, nobody dared to say 'no' to any demand of the "master". Injustice, discrimination, and being subject to cruel treatment was the norm. The above-mentioned scenario prevailed when the Vidhayak Sansad began operating in the area. The Vidhayak Sansad based its ideology on the Gandhian principle of non-violence as a strategy for social change. The core belief of the organisation was and is "Cooperate where you can and resist where you must".

While carrying out their work, they faced strong opposition from the elite of the society, including the moneylenders and landowners, but this did not deter them. Through their efforts, the people got together and helped in releasing bonded labourers. There were incidents of attacks by local authorities, but the supporters of the causes protected them.

Aims and Objectives of the Vidhayak Sansad

The aims and objectives of the Vidhayak Sansad are as follows:

(a) To spread education, including health education through constructive and welfare activities.
(b) To bring about economic and social upliftment of the rural poor and hutment dwellers.
(c) To establish social justice through constitutional ways and means.
(d) To educate the poor about the fundamental rights enshrined in the Constitution of India.
(e) To help release and rehabilitate the bonded labourers and solve their problems.
(f) To organise training programmes, legal-aid centres, and implement the projects intended for economic development of the downtrodden.

Development in Practice

Rehabilitation of freed bonded labourers was a major focus of the Vidhayak Sansad. With this objective, they initiated the following programmes and activities:

- Conscientisation
- Capacity-building
- Village watershed development
- Agricultural development and land reforms
- Educational development
- Bhonga Shala (school under a thatched roof), Mukta Shala (temporary seasonal school), and Shibir Shala (residential school)
- Centre for Budget Studies
- Warli Art Gallery
- Healthcare activities
- Sponsorship and community development

Schooling Programme

The right to education is the fundamental right stated/ guaranteed in Article 45 of the Constitution. It states that "the State shall endeavour to provide, within a period of 10 years from the commencement of this Constitution, for free and compulsory education for all children until they complete the age of fourteen years". The state could not achieve this goal even after 65 years of independence and access to education for the marginalised was not achieved.

To implement and monitor the government programmes and make the government accountable, a survey was conducted by the Vidhayak Sansad in the three talukas of Bhiwandi, Wada, and Shahapur in Thane district. The survey found that approximately 2,400 children were out of school in the selected 300 hamlets (*padas*). Hence, in order to provide education for the deprived children, Vidhayak Sansad started a schooling revolution in the district through establishing various formal and non-formal educational facilities for *adivasis* and ex-untouchable children. These activities were initiated in 1995-1996 with the aim of reducing child labour and increasing the number of school-going children. With regard to child labour, special schools for elementary education were also started. The Vidhayak Sansad initiated a mobile library, a science exhibition, Warli art camps, celebration of national festivals, plantation, recreation, sport assemblage, and training camps for the *adivasis*. Different kinds of schools for the out-of-school children were also started: Bhonga Shala, Mukta Shala, Shibir Shala, and Study Classes. Details of these are provided in the following section. At the same time, the Vidhayak Sansad continued to pressurise the government to implement education programmes in the rural areas.

The Bhonga Shala (a school under a thatched roof)

As noted previously, a large number of people migrated each year for a period of up to 6 months in the lean period. Such migrations were regular in the talukas of Jawahar, Wada, Mokhada, Talasari, and Vikramgarh and migrants would go to Vasai, Bhiwandi, and Thane to work in brick-kilns.

A Bhonga Shala is a special school for the children of the migrant workers in the brick-kiln industries. Bhonga Shalas have temporary structures and are built on the land belonging to the villagers. The Bhonga Shalas are built collectively by the members of the Sanghatana, local people, and teachers. The idea of collectivity ensures sharing of responsibility and feeling of ownership of the programmes.

Each Bhonga Shala has classrooms from the 1st to the 4th standards. Each class has 25 students and a teacher. Teachers stay at the school day and night for six months. Only lady teachers from the concerned villages or neighbouring villages are appointed. Teachers are required to assemble the children daily and bring them to school as well as drop them back to their homes. Initially the gathered children would often run away. An additional responsibility of the Vidhayak Sansad teachers is to ensure hygiene of the children. These factors make the work of the teachers challenging, the major challenge being sustaining attendance levels. The periodical progressive performance of the Bhonga Shalas is presented in Table 2.1.

The Mukta Shala (Temporary Seasonal School)

According to the National Education Scheme, 1998, and the State Plan of Action, 1994, for universalising education, the Mukta Shala is the best option where the other education schemes are not available. The scheme of Mukta Shala was suggested to the state government for implementation by the Vidhayak Sansad, but it has not been implemented till 2006. The state government

Table 2.1: Bhonga Shala Project of the Vidhayak Sansad

Sr. No.	*Years*	*No. of Centres*	*No. of Teachers*	*No. of Students*	*Exam*	*Pass*	*Percentage*
1	1995-96	25	25	457	255	218	85.49
2	1996-97	52	52	1133	662	590	89.12
3	1997-98	81	81	2093	967	827	85.52
4	1998-99	82	82	2080	1015	922	90.83
5	1999-00	115	115	2784	1481	1424	96.15
6	2000-01	143	143	3169	1785	1690	94.67
7	2001-02	152	152	2948	1768	1658	93.77
8	2002-03	145	145	3087	1686	1554	92.17
9	2003-04	256	256	5086	3009	2787	92.68
10	2004-05	221	221	4265	2710	2553	94.20
11	2005-06	125	125	2693	1853	1758	94.87

Source: Education Department of the Vidhayak Sansad, 2007.

formed a task force committee, that included Vivek Pandit (Samarthan),[8] Dilip Gogate (Asst. Director of Primary Education) and Vijaya Chauhan (UNICEF). It was recommended that to promote and enable the Mukta Shala was the responsibility of the Zilla Parishad, District Education Officer, Collector, Tribal Welfare Development, and NGOs. However, the state government did not provide funds to implement this scheme.

The Shibir Shala (Residential School)

The Shibir Shala is an opportunity for children from economically backward classes of society. The aim of this school is to provide education to those who have no access to education on their own and those who are very far from mainstream society. The school is residential and for the children belonging to the age group between 9 and 15 years. This school provides a variety of educational equipment. The school provides an opportunity especially for the tribals with priority to Katkari, Thakar, and Warli tribes. The first Shibir Shala was started in January 2001 at Usgaon. A course has been designed including a syllabus on a par with the 7th standard and the goal is to enable the children to pass the 7th standard and join the mainstream schools from the 8th standard. The course is for the period of 18 months.

The Agriculture Development Programme

From 1982 till the time the study was conducted in 2006, about 1,200 bonded labourers had been freed. The newly achieved freedom led to the issue of their rehabilitation which was a challenging issue. The released bonded labourers had no source of income. Very few of them had their own funds. Around 40% of the bonded labourers were marginal farmers and the rest were landless labourers. Agriculture in tribal areas is characterised by low technology and irrigation facilities intend to be extremely inadequate. Owing to inadequate irrigation facilities and low productivity of land, the production from their lands was not sufficient for the survival of their families for the whole year. Most were unable to cultivate a second crop and other kinds of cash crops.

The state government was supposed to provide cash assistance and to allocate lands for cultivation to the released bonded labourers, but none received this benefit. Another major reason to focus on agricultural development was the seasonal migration of people to other cities in search of employment. Though there may be no apparent direct link between agricultural practices and migration, the starting of the new crop helped to reduce migration. Hence an agricultural development programme became essential. The programme was launched in 1983-84 in Vasai taluka for the rehabilitation of freed bonded labourers. The dream of freed bonded labourers was to develop agriculture for their own consumption and get adequate food. Keeping this in mind, the Vidhayak Sansad initiated activities such as grain banks, fertiliser supply centres, collective farming to cultivate watermelon, groundnut, green fodder and centre for research of the variety of rice and fruits.

The Crop Credit Programme

The crop credit programme is a major activity of the agriculture department. The idea of a crop credit programme was to provide credit to poor and needy marginal farmers. One of the major problems of the farmers was the availability of food grains, seeds, fertilizers, and other agricultural material. Naturally, they had to take loans with high interests from moneylenders. Also, they had to borrow the *khawati*[9] which made them indebted for years. To find a solution to this problem the Vidhayak Sansad started the crop credit programme, which ensured that people get seeds and fertilizers on time and would not have to go to the moneylenders for loan.

This crop credit was given to the growers of both Rabi and Kharif crops. The credit was given in the form of required seeds, fertilisers, pesticides, etc.

A majority of the organisation's members were landless and worked on brick-kilns, often migrating to cities, viz. Surat, Mumbai, Ratnagiri and Raigadh in search of a livelihood. In other areas, where irrigation was available and a few members owned land, efforts for agricultural development were made.

The Watershed Development Programme

The Watershed development programme was started in 1991 to rehabilitate freed bonded labourers and to develop agricultural activities. The main aim of the programme was to help marginal farmers, farm-workers, and the landless to get employment. Another aim of this programme was to facilitate natural resource management. Soil conservation and water conservation were major activities under the programme. These bring about permanent improvement in the land resources and help in preserving moisture in the soil for a long period, especially in the areas where agriculture is rain-fed. Land treatment measures have resulted in an increase in the area brought under cultivation by the beneficiaries. Beneficiaries in all villages covered by the programme obtained higher average yields for crops and were able to take up a second crop and co-operative farming. Also, they could grow vegetable and fruit plants. Their lands have become more fertile and some members could take up double cropping.

The watershed programme helped not only to raise the productivity of land of the beneficiaries but also to generate employment within the village during the lean season. This resulted in changes in the behaviour of other communities towards the tribal community. The *Patils'* behaviour towards them changed. Most of the people reported that the *Patils* used to previously beat and abuse them, but this changed and while some *Patils* became indifferent, others improved their manner of talking to the freed bonded labourers. Freed bonded labourers often shared food with *Patils*. Previously, shop owners did not give them grain on credit, but later did so as they felt assured of repayment.

Creating Linkages

The efficiency of any policy primarily depends on the budgetary allocation towards the programmes. As mentioned previously, one of the Vidhayak Sansad's programmes is the Centre for Budget Studies. This programme helped to bridge the gap between the grassroots and the upper levels of governance. The Centre provides information to the grassroots which enables them to make the right demands and negotiate effectively. Many social action groups like Shramjeevi Sanghatana and others became aware about the allocation of budget and were able to put forth their demands to the right authorities, using the information to support their cause. Thus, Samarthan, a Mumbai-based advocacy centre works as a support organisation for grassroots and state-level organisations and helps the Vidhyak Sansad to advocate issues and articulate demands to be placed before the government.

5B. Profile of the Shramjeevi Sanghatana

The Shramjeevi Sanghatana is a people's organisation registered as a Trade Union with Vidyullata Pandit as its founder president. It was founded on October 21, 1982 at village Dahisar, Thane district. The Sanghatana works in close coordination with the Vidhayak Sansad. The Sanghatana is known as an organisation of *adivasis* and of freed bonded labourers, and has launched struggles against slavery, injustice, exploitation, and other inhuman practices.

After freeing bonded labourers, the Vidhayak Sansad envisaged the need for an organised effort to combat entrenched power structures such as *Patils*, moneylenders, landlords, and politicians. Such an organised effort is possible only with active participation of the people. During the course of freeing bonded labourers, the Sanghatana faced confrontation with established powers but once it was able to mobilise and organise people, the task became self-sustaining.

The Shramjeevi Sanghatana, is a membership-based organisation, while the Vidhayak Sansad is the grassroots development organisation involved in creating enabling conditions for the empowerment of the people with its well-designed and efficiently managed programmes to strengthen education, health, and livelihood among the most marginalised people. The Sanghatana works at strengthening the leadership abilities of tribal youth, men, and women. It is a trade union helping people to assert their rights.[10] For example, the Sanghatana empowered its members to obtain entitlement certificates of lands they cultivated. The Sanghatana also addresses issues such as atrocities on women and *adivasis* and helps with obtaining a caste certificate, PDS, safe drinking water, roads, electricity, and implementation of other civic amenities for the people.

During the time of the study in 2007, the Sanghatana had over 15,000 members in the area. The Sanghatana covered 450 hamlets/villages with 240 village committees at the village level.

Strategic Intervention

"Cooperate where you can and resist where you must." This slogan of the Shramjeevi Sanghatana is based on Gandhian philosophy. The leaders only use the weapon of struggle for their rights when other approaches have failed. Their weapon is non-violent and constitutional in nature. The Sanghatana's organisational structure and function is different from that of the Sansad.

The following section focuses on its structure and activities.

Structure of Shramjeevi Sanghatana

The structure of the Shramjeevi Sanghatana is different from the structure of the Vidhayak Sansad. The hierarchy of its structure is described below.

Executive Committee

The general body elects the members of the Executive Committee. The Executive Committee is the soul of the Shramjeevi Sanghatana. All the important decisions are taken in the monthly executive meeting. The Sanghatana is responsible for the overall planning and implementation. Through meetings the programmes are planned for the district level, taluka level, zone level (zone comprises eight to eleven villages), and village level activities. Certain regular programmes are planned at the central level include training of activists, details of planning, public meetings, collective celebrations like national days, including Independence Day, Republic Day, death and birth anniversaries of legendary personalities and reformers; celebration of some important days like science day, human rights day, international women's day, bal din (Children's day), etc.

One of the important activities is preservation of the *adivasi* culture. Folk dance and singing is therefore encouraged through the *Nach Melawa,* for the various tribal groups such as Warli, Malhar Koli, Thakar, Katkari, and Kokana. The aim of these celebrations is social interaction to strengthen contacts and to enhance integration, solidarity, and communication amongst members and activists as well as others. Through meetings the programmes are planned at the district level, taluka level, zone level (zone comprises eight to eleven villages), and the village level.

Taluka Committee

Since each Taluka (block) has its own typical set of problems, the Taluka Committtee is an important part of the structure of Shramjeevi Sanghatana. This Committee is the important centre of leadership in the Block. The Committee participates in the District Executive meeting, during which it presents a report to the Shramjeevi Sanghatana.

Generally, the Taluka Secretaries have a clear perspective, knowledge, and perception about the local issues. They are sharp, competent and skilled at arranging *dharna*s, *morcha*s, rallies, and campaigns involving confrontation and cooperation. Taluka Secretaries are the first cadre activists. They are sufficiently articulate and clear about their roles and responsibilities to facilitate the organisation and its advocacy campaign at various levels.

Zonal Committee

This Committee is formed by members of village-level activists. The Zonal Committee represents a group of 8 to 11 villages forming a cluster. It handles complex cases of the people. It is the mediator between the Village Committee and the Taluka Committee.

Village Committee

The Village Committee Head's task involves getting new members so as to strengthen the Sanghatana. The members of this Committee are elected to solve village-level problems and disputes in a just manner. Their role is to help make villagers aware of their rights. The Village Committee looks after a group of 7 to 9 hamlets (*padas*).

Functioning

Various levels of the Sanghatana have close coordination with one another. The structure of the Sanghatana is its strength and is reflected in its capacity to accept challenges, to respond, and to succeed. It is a close-knit network useful for spreading any message amongst its members.

Some crucial activities undertaken by the Sanghatana are described below.

Bonded Labour Release Programme

The inhuman practice of bonded labour was rampant in Thane district even post-independence. However, the government claimed that there was not a single bonded labourer in the state, but, the Shramjeevi Sanghatana established that bonded labour still existed in Thane and helped to make the government accountable. The Sanghatana helped release 1,200-bonded labourers from the practices of *Lagingadi* (the practice of holding bonded labour to repay the loan for marriage) and fishing bondage (wherein the people were forced to do fishing for a meagre amount). The Sanghatana filed cases against 465 "masters", *Patils*, and moneylenders. It was for the first time in India that the "masters" got arrested for holding bonded labourers.

Struggles for Flag Hoisting: Celebrating a Great Heritage

The struggle to host a flag hoisting function is a landmark incident in the history of the Shramjeevi Sanghatana. On August 15, 1983, freed bonded labourers from Depivali village carried out flag hoisting, but only after serious confrontation with the police, the government, and elite members of the society. The *adivasis* were arrested but were resolute about carrying out the flag hoisting. They have been carrying out flag hoisting on August 15 in the subsequent years as well. Each year, members get together at Akoli and Ganeshpuri villages and hold rallies. As many as 15,000 people participate in the event each year.

Struggle for Minimum Wages

The struggle for minimum wages is another important campaign undertaken by the Sanghatana. The Sanghatana highlighted the issue of minimum wages through the media and other mechanisms. The Sanghatana fought against Gurudev Siddhapeeth (an Ashram) in Ganeshpuri. Foreigners used to visit the Ashram and *adivasis* worked there but the Ashram did not pay minimum wages as per the rules of government. Moreover, women did not receive equal wages.

Therefore, the Sanghatana got into confrontation with the Ashram. It held a meeting at the main gate of the Ashram on April 19, 1987. The Sanghatana members went on strike for 33 days. They held *morchas* and *dharanas* and carried out a non-violent struggle. Through these efforts, the tribals began to be paid minimum wages by the Ashram.

The struggle for minimum wages was replicated in several villages, viz. Devghar, Tilher, Budhawali, Sarashol,Wageghar, Kanchad and Kalamkhand. People were paid in kind (getting clothes along with a rupee or two for the whole year). *Adivasis* did not know about the Act, which assured Rs. 7 per day for eight hours of work at that time. The Sanghatana carried out the struggle for minimum wages in several villages, viz. Devghar, Tilher, Budhawali, Sarashol,Wageghar, Kanchad and Kalamkhand. Along with the campaign for minimum wages, the Sanghatana also engaged in another campaign for 'equal pay for equal work'. There was a difference in the wage rates of men and women and men received Rs. 5 per day while women received Rs. 2 for the same work.

In many of the villages, changes occurred through the efforts of the Sanghatana. One such village, Tilher, was identified for the detailed study.

6. The Objectives

The organisations selected for this study are active Voluntary Organisations, which illustrate the development initiative as a process of social transformation. The broader objective is to understand the conscientisation strategies, their effectiveness in building rights-based organisations and mobilisation of the people in government programmes and influencing government agencies for evolving and implementing people-centred policies and programmes. The specific objectives are as follows:

1. To examine the conscientisation role of selected Voluntary Organisations in the development initiative of the *adivasis* in Thane District.
2. To observe the impact on the members of the organisations in making the government administration accountable for implementing the programmes devised for the socio-economic development of *adivasis* and other marginalised sections of society.
3. To assess people's response to the development programmes.
4. To examine the benefits and impact on families/ households in the village under study through individual members of the organisations.

7. The Hypotheses

Since the Vidhayak Sansad and the Shramjeevi Sanghatana are engaged in conscientising the *adivasi* members of their organisations, the role of conscientisation has been considered significant in organising the development initiative, and accordingly, the following hypotheses have been formulated:

1. The educative role of NGOs in the sub-region has resulted in the emergence of autonomous leadership among the *adivasis*.

2. With the enlightenment of the members of the target communities/groups, they have become assertive in exercising their rights.
3. With the assertion of rights, people have made the government machinery active to implement the government schemes meant for socio-economic development of *adivasis*.
4. The development initiative of the conscientised *adivasis* helped bringing about change in the socio-economic status of *adivasis* in general.

As conscientisation is the main concept, the author has followed Paulo Freire's formulation as the theoretical framework for this study.

8. Theoretical Framework: Conscientisation: An Instrument of Liberation

For undertaking a study on the development initiative by *adivasis* in Thane district, *Pedagogy of the Oppressed* (1970) by Paulo Freire has been considered as the framework. Freire emphasised *conscientisation* throughout his pedagogy. According to Freire, 'the term conscientisation refers to learning to perceive social, political, and economic contradictions and to take action against the oppressive elements of reality'. [11] It is a process of 'awakening of critical consciousness' [12] by developing pedagogy of the oppressed. The task of awakening has to be carried out by the radicals. The initial stage, therefore, is to deal with the problem of consciousness of the oppressed to 'wage the struggle to resolve the contradiction in which they are caught'.[13]

Freire viewed his pedagogy as 'the only effective instrument in which the revolutionary leadership establishes a permanent relationship of dialogue with the oppressed'.[14] By dialogue, he means the engagement of dialoguers 'in critical thinking,'[15] which includes action.[16] Action constitutes 'the present, existential, concrete situation, reflecting the aspirations of the people'.[17]

In his pedagogy, Freire sees the importance of 'leadership training courses'[18] to give the status of leaders. Further, he developed a theory of dialogical action. His theory constitutes the elements of cooperation, unity of the oppressed individuals for liberation, and organisation. According to Freire, cooperation can be 'achieved though communication'.[19] Unity, he thought, was essential both in the revolutionary leaders and in the people. For achieving unity, raising of class-consciousness is essential. Organisation, according to him is 'a highly educational process in which, leaders and people together experience true authority and freedom'.[20]

So it is pertinent to quote what Richard Shaull contended in his Foreword to Freire's work that it is 'contribution to the education of illiterate adults in the Third World'.[21] Considering Freire's *Pedagogy of the Oppressed* as a revolutionary instrument of social transformation, it is applied to examine the impact of the role of conscientisation of the *adivasi* members both by the Vidhayak Sansad and the Shramjeevi Sanghatana in the development initiatives.

9. Selection of Respondents

In 2007, the Vidhayak Sansad and the Shramjeevi Sanghatana operated in 10 talukas and in more than 200 villages (about 450 padas/hamlets) in Thane district. The membership at the time was over 15,000. The author selected 70 members (50%) for the interviews out of 140 members from the study village. Selection was done such that all women members (100%) were covered. The author held discussions with members and activists who worked at village, taluka, and district levels and with some non-members as well.

Selection of respondents was based on the taluka-wise list of members, activists, beneficiaries, and local people's representatives. Since the focus of the study was to examine the role of both organisations towards socio-economic changes among the *adivasis*, the members of organisations with more than 10 years of membership were identified as respondents. The respondents were grassroots activists. The author carried out periodic comparison, i.e. before the intervention and after the intervention of organisations in the study areas. An attempt was made to investigate the level of awareness, social development, and empowerment where the organisations operated vis-à-vis areas where they did not. The variables of caste, community, and gender balance were taken account of while selecting the respondents. For studying the situation where the activities of the organisations were absent, a control village was identified. Table 2.2 provides details of selection of respondents. The data have been revised in March 2015.

Table 2.2: Selection of Respondents

Sr. No.	*Particulars*	*Numbers*
1.	Total population of selected village	3,690
2.	Total households of selected village	792
3.	Total Scheduled Tribes population of village	3,406
4.	Total members of the organisations	140
5.	Selected members of the organisations	70 (50.0)
6.	Female members	16 (22.9)
	Male members	54 (77.1)
7.	Pada-wise selection of members	
	Varthapada	12 (17.1)
	Tilher	6 (8.6)
	Jadhavpada	15 (21.4)
	Kuwarp ada	24 (34.3)
	Khairpada	5 (7.1)
	Palipada	4 (5.7)
	Burudpada	1 (1.4)
	Dhumalpada	3 (4.3)
	Total	70 (100.0)
8.	The Tribe of members	
	Warli	40 (57.1)
	Malhar Koli	20 (28.6)
	Ma Thakur	6 (8.6)
	Katkari	4 (5.7)
	Total	70 (100.0)

10. Sources of Data

Two kinds of data were used for the study. The data were obtained from the following two sources:

1. Sources for secondary data are as follows:
    - Annual reports of both organisations under study
    - Government reports published by the Ministry of Tribal Affairs and Tribal Commission, etc.

- Census Reports and Gazetteer with special reference to Thane district
- Survey and Evaluation Reports, viz. National Sample Survey and Human Development Reports, etc.

2. Primary data were gathered from the following:
    - Member activists of the organisations under study
    - Founder members of the organisations
    - Members of the organisations
    - Local representatives such as the Sarpanch and Gram Panchayat members of the village

For additional information, known social activists in the area, grassroots activists, local leaders, community workers, school teachers, *gram sevaks,* and others were contacted for discussing certain issues. These efforts helped the author to sharpen the ideas about work and experience of Voluntary Organisations.

11. Strategy of Data Collection

For collecting primary data, a strategy of developing a good rapport with the founders of both organisations and member activists was adopted. This was easy because the author had worked in one of the organisations. The data were collected from the organisations' anecdotes, focus group discussions, and individual interactions with previous and present activists, members, and staff. After constructing an in-depth interview schedule, primary data were collected through personal interviews of the respondents. The interview timings were set according to the convenience of respondents. The author made efforts to interview respondents on their farmlands. Initially, respondents were not so open but after staying with them for some days, they opened up and came up with frank responses. Also, after staying in villages and having meetings with activists they were assured as their queries were answered. The author had the opportunity to stay with *adivasis* in hamlets and closely observe the programmes as well as hold discussions with lay persons.

An in-depth interview schedule was constructed to collect the data from the select respondents, who were members of the organisations. In the interviews the following items were in focus:

- Socio-economic background of the respondents
- Individual information of the respondents
- Their family background and education
- Standard of living
- Occupation and chances of mobility
- Agricultural information with regard to ownership, cropping pattern, etc.
- Economic condition
- Marriage and network of social relationship
- Ideological commitment and political affiliation
- Cultural practices, particularly folkways (folk traditions)
- Social awareness
- Information about the organisations and their membership
- Awareness about Tribal–Sub Plan schemes
- Development schemes of organisations
- Action programmes

The author collected data within 2 months, i.e. November-December 2006. This period was suitable for the villagers. Consultations with activists and leaders helped in collecting data. It took almost an hour to interview the activists of both organisations. The author visited the offices of organisations and the villages under study where the income-generation programmes were undertaken and the bonded labourers struggled against their landlords and moneylenders. Also, the technique of participation in some of the programmes was adopted. This helped to learn about their past history and involvement with the organisations. It was useful in obtaining first-hand information of their views of social development and empowerment programmes. Many times, the author had personal dialogues with the founder members of the organisations about their programmes. Besides, a discussion method with the group of activists was used for better understanding the strategies of organisations. In order to get in-depth knowledge, the author participated on special occasions such as community celebrations, national celebrations and their cultural events like folk dances, folk songs, and so on. Also, the author participated in various demonstrations, including *dharana, morcha* and visits to government officers.

12. Key Terms/Concepts in the Study

In this study, key terms/concepts such as Voluntary Organisation, voluntary action, social development, people's participation in development, empowerment, and advocacy have been used. Their meanings both in the social science theory and applied in this study have been spelled out as follows:

Voluntary Organisation

The term Voluntary Organisation is synonymous with NGO. It is also referred to as voluntary agency, social work agency, social action, people's movement group, religious group, community development organisation, non-party group, or a charitable trust. Voluntary organisations may be registered as societies or as charitable trusts, under the central or state laws. Some states have adopted the Societies Registration Act (1860). A voluntary organisation is a group organised for the pursuit of one or several interests in common. The group is organised on the basis of voluntary membership that is neither mandatory nor gained through birth, but is purely voluntary. It is usually initiated spontaneously, at least at the level of those who form it and governed by its members without any external control.[22]

A Voluntary Organisation is a group of people who have organised themselves as a legal corporate body to render social services through organised efforts. Lord Beveridge defined Voluntary Organisation as *an organisation in which whether its workers are paid or unpaid is initiated and governed by its own members without external control.*[23] Another definition of Voluntary Organisation by D.K. Sills, explains that it is *a group of persons organised on the basis of voluntary membership without state control for the furtherance of some common interests of its members.*[24] For the purpose of the study, the term *Voluntary Organisation* has been used in the sense of an autonomous agency, which renders social service.

Voluntary Action

Voluntary action implies action that has common goals and collective action. Voluntary action can be carried out without registration under the charity commissioner, and can mobilise its resources within the group. Mostly voluntary action does not rely on foreign financial assistance. Voluntary action is the common goal of Voluntary Organisations and people's organisations. The concept of *voluntary action* has become very popular in the last three decades. Conceptually, *any action by an individual, an informal group, or a duly constituted organisation, which is not promoted by external pressure or self-interest, can be termed 'voluntary action'*.[25] Voluntary action is synonymous with community action, people's organisation, social activity, social activist, action group, voluntary agency, non-governmental organisation, non-party political process, or non-political formation.[26] The classification of action groups is based on the type of activities it undertakes, i.e. relief and charity; trade unions, development-oriented; mobilisation and organisation; politics and political education. Mostly, the action groups are engaged in organising, mobilising, and conscientisation of the oppressed. The author preferred the voluntary action concept because it is applicable to selected people's organisations for the study.

Social Development

Here, the conception of social development is based on the analysis given by S.L. Sharma. In the context of the Indian experience through the model of the Constitution of India, we find four conceptions of social development: (i) increase in social well-being, (ii) being free from exploitation and oppression, (iii) securing social justice, and (iv) bringing about social integration. The first refers to several provisions of social services such as health, education, housing, employment and social security. It is about getting economic benefits. The second pertains to the abolition of the practice of bonded labour. The third involves the treatment of equality, preferential allocation and distribution of goods/resources, equality of opportunity and empowerment. It has been formulated in the interest of Scheduled Castes,

Scheduled Tribes, and other disadvantaged and deprived sections. For this, special policies are evolved. The last 'social integration' is viewed in terms of equal relationship with any person or community. Legalising intermarriages, ending discriminatory practices under the principle of equality before law, increasing political participation of the members of Scheduled Castes, Scheduled Tribes, and Muslim communities in politics and governments at all levels, etc. are examples of some attempts to achieve social integration.[27] While taking an appraisal of efforts both by government and NGOs, these above-mentioned four conceptions of social development have been viewed for the development of *adivasis* in Thane district.

Empowerment

There are many initiatives of empowerment strategies that have been initiated by poor people themselves, government, civil society organisations and non-state actors. The World Bank's Empowerment Sourcebook (2002) defines, *empowerment is the process of enhancing the capacity of individuals or groups to make choices and to transform those choices into desired actions and outcomes.*[28] Central to this process are actions, which build both individual and collective assets, and improve the efficiency and fairness of the organisational and institutional context which govern the use of these assets. The essence of empowerment is the self-determined change. The implications of policies, programmes and activities that empower poor people and those are expected to enhance development choices, and improve people's quality of life. According to Bina Agarwal, it is a process that *enhances the ability of disadvantaged (powerless) individuals or groups to challenge and change (in their favour) existing power relationships that place them in subordinate economic, social, and political positions.*[29] Empowerment, thus, is a process of enhancing the ability of powerless individuals/groups aimed at changing the socio-economic and political status of the marginalised, ex-untouchables, *adivasis*, women and other disadvantaged. In this sense, the term empowerment has been conceived for empirical observation on the *adivasi* activists' initiative in the village under study.

People-centred Advocacy

The term advocacy is suitable for the study for the reason that both the organisations strengthened the real process of advocacy in India and abroad with its organising and mobilising activities. The term advocacy means amplifying the voice of the voiceless. It is very popular in India since the last two decades. According to John Samuel, *Advocacy is a well-organised process to influencing decision-makers to design, adopt, and change policies and practices for the deprived people.*[30] There is a comprehensive definition by David Cohen on advocacy that is, *organised efforts and actions that use the instruments of democracy to strengthen the democratic process. These instruments can include elections, lobbying, mass mobilisations, civil disobedience, negotiations/bargaining, and court actions. Efforts and actions are designed to persuade and influence those who hold governmental, political, and economic power so that they will formulate, adopt, and implement public policy in ways that improve the lives of those with less conventional political power and fewer economic resources. Advocacy has a purposeful result: to change society's institutions as well as the power relationships within and among the institutions such that those with less conventional political power and fewer economic resources acquire a greater share of each.*[31]

Some examples of advocacy include: the right to food movement, the silent valley project for the abolition of Bonded Labour Act (1976), or the Right to Information and National Rural Employment Guarantee Act. People-centred advocacy has its roots in the Indian Constitution and Human Rights. The role of advocacy is very important in this changing global era and is the new mantra of development, which implies the existence of a larger market and minimum government, to make governance accountable for the poor. People-centred advocacy is a set of organised actions aimed at influencing public policies, societal attitudes, and socio-political processes that enable and empower the marginalised to speak for themselves. Its purpose is social transformation through the realisation of human rights: civil, political, economic, social and cultural. Hence, it is the spirit of democracy that drives the very idea of people-centred advocacy.

In the context of this study, people-centred advocacy refers to amplifying the voice of *adivasis* to the decision-makers and rights-based organising and mobilising activists to assert their rights.

To conclude, this chapter aimed at presenting the research design of the study. It discussed the locale of the study and the socio-political status of the Thane district. It discussed emergence of the organisations, their objectives and landmark achievements in the backdrop of voluntary action in the area. Their work of conscientisation and liberation with *adivasis* and their approach to work with the communities was discussed.

The next (third) chapter deals with the profile of members. As a result of the conscientisation by both organisations, many *adivasis* became activists. Their socio-economic background, their enlightenment level, etc. are important aspects, which are described in the next chapter.

NOTES

1. Government of India: Ministry of Tribal Affairs, *Programmes for Promotion of Voluntary Action, Annual Report 2005-2006*, New Delhi, 2006, p. 95.
2. Mishra, Neeraj: The Noose Tightens, *India Today*, New Delhi, January 29, 2007, p. 34.
3. Jain R.B.: NGOs as the Non-State Actor in Public Administration, *Public Administration in India*, Deep and Deep, New Delhi, 2002.
4. http:/www.census2011.co.in/demographic status of scheduled tribe population of India.
5. Government of Maharashtra: *Gazetteer of the Bombay Presidency, Thana Places of Interest*, Gazetteers Department, Bombay, 2000, p. 335.
6. Parulekar, Godavari: *Jhevha Manoos Jaga Hoto*, Mauj Prakashan, Mumbai, 1999.
7. http:/www.census2011.co.in/census/district/355-thane.html.
8. Samarthan is a state advocacy centre based in Mumbai and advocating the budget rights of the marginalised in Maharashtra and linking struggles micro to macro through the decision-makers and media.
9. *Khawati*: The practice of taking *khawati* or consumption loan from *Patils* was prevalent in the area. The mode of charging interest involves doubling the loan amount given in a one-year period. Given this exorbitant rate of interest, borrowers tend to fall into a debt trap whereby they end up cultivating crops and using all the earnings only to repay the *khawati*. To combat this, the Sanstha

decided to start extending *khawati* at reasonable rates along with the crop credit programme. It was observed that only those who were needy responded and others continued to borrow from someone else.

10. Pandit, Vivek: *Fearless Minds*, National Centre for Advocacy Studies, Pune, 2000.
11. Freire, Paulo: *Pedagogy of the Oppressed*, Penguin, Harmondsworth, 1996, p. 17.
12. Ibid., p. 18.
13. Ibid., p. 38.
14. Ibid., p. 50.
15. Ibid., p. 73.
16. Ibid.
17. Ibid., p. 76.
18. Ibid., p. 123.
19. Ibid., p. 149.
20. Ibid., pp. 159-60.
21. Ibid., p. 11.
22. Sooryamoorthy, R. and Gangrade, K.D.: *NGOs in India*, Rawat Publications, New Delhi, 2006, p. 24.
23. Mohanty, Manoranjan and Singh, Anil K.: *Voluntarism and Government*, Voluntary Action Network India, New Delhi, 2001, p. 19.
24. Ibid.
25. Dantwala, M.L.: *Promises to Keep*, in Dantwala, M.L., Sethi, Harsh and Visaria, Pravin (eds.), *Social Change Through Voluntary Action*, Sage Publications, New Delhi, 1998, p. 31.
26. Dhanagare, D.N.: *Themes and Perspectives in Indian Sociology*, Rawat Publications, New Delhi, 1993, pp. 155-165.
27. Sharma, S.L.: Social Development: Reflections on the Concept and the Indian Experience, *Guru Nanak Journal of Sociology*, Vol. 10, Nos. 1-2, April-October, 1989, pp. 37-55.
28. www. http://go.worldbank.org/WXKIV52RBO.
29. Agarwal, Bina: *A Field of One's Own, Gender and Land Rights in South Asia*, Cambridge University Press, New Delhi, 1994, p. 39.
30. National Centre for Advocacy Studies: *Draft Paper on Understanding Advocacy*, Pune, 2006.
31. Cohen, David: *The Elements of Advocacy in Resource Kit for Advocacy and Campaign Building*, National Centre for Advocacy Studies, Pune, 1996, p. 13.

3

The Socio-economic Profile of the Members of the Organisations

1. Introduction

The last chapter discussed the profile of the organisations and the research design of the study. The socio-demographic profile of the households, the membership of the 'Sanghatana', and the subsequent benefits are portrayed in this chapter. It is expected that the data on the members' socio-economic profile will demonstrate the significant changes in their lives that resulted from the organisations' efforts. Similarly, the information on the benefits of government schemes, social relations, participation in political processes, etc., will indicate advantages gained on fronts other than the livelihood issues. The present chapter, therefore, draws attention to the socio-economic background of the *adivasi* respondents before joining the organisations, the changes brought about in their socio-economic status, and the degree of participation in the local government after joining the organisations.

Thane district is well known for its *adivasi* culture, mainly for its Warli art. The Warli art has reached the global level owing to the efforts of civil society organisations. Twenty-two per cent of *adivasis* are Scheduled Tribes in the Thane district. According to the Scheduled Castes and Scheduled Tribes Commission, 91% of *adivasis* were below the poverty line.[1]

2. The Socio-Economic Condition of the *Adivasis* in Thane District

The Scheduled Area notified by the Government of India

consists of 5,691 villages and 12 districts in 73 blocks, 16.5% of the state area. These districts are Thane, Pune, Nashik, Dhule, Nandurbar, Jalgaon, Ahmednagar, Nanded, Amaravati, Yeotmal, Gadchiroli, and Chandrapur. There are 47 Scheduled Tribes in Maharashtra state. Three of these were declared as primitive tribes, i.e. Katkari, Kolam, and Gond. Thane district has a large number of *adivasi*s (i.e. 14.7%) of the population. The *adivasis* in Thane district are Warli, Katkari, Kathodi, Malhar Koli, Mahadev Koli, and Mathakur.

The following paragraph describes the condition of *adivasi*s around the 1980s, i.e. before the emergence of the organisations.

Thane district was known for its forests and for *adivasi*s with their rich culture. Though it was known for rich natural resources, there was widespread extension of urbanisation, an extension of Mumbai sub-urban. The district is the source of raw material supply to Mumbai. The landlords, moneylenders, and timber traders were self-declared forest contractors who employed *adivasis* for felling trees and clearing forests for their business. *Adivasis* were deprived of assets and were dependent for their livelihood on others due to absence of a livelihood source. Often evicted in the name of forest development and conservation by the foresters, their survival depended on gathering fruits, honey, or on hunting and collecting other available edible items.

Warkas (slope and plain) lands and *jagirdari* (a practice of holding of lands or revenues assigned by the state) were the major issues connected with the *adivasis*. *Jagirdars* used to give plain and slopes lands for paddy cultivation to *adivasis* on a permanent basis. Cultivation was done after clearing the forest area. The *adivasis* had to pay a fixed amount to the *jagirdars*. No land records of these lands were maintained. After the abolition of *jagirdari*, paddy fields were recorded in the name of people but *Warkas* lands were left out knowingly. It is said that in Thane district alone there were more than one lakh acres of *Warkas* land on which thousands of *adivasis* subsisted.[2]

Apart from this, there were other problems related to lands. These included *Eksali* land (the *Eksali* scheme was meant for the cultivation in forest lands for the survival of *adivasis* and ex-untouchables) problems, regularisation of forest lands, and reclaiming lands from the "masters" for freed bonded labourers. There were two major conditions while cultivating the *Eksali* lands, i.e. cultivators could not claim entitlement or *Patta* and could not apply for ration cards. On account of these conditions, they had no official status and hence tended to be more deprived. Also, there was no political will to solve their land problems. The landlords used their power over the *adivasis* to extract forced labour or *veth*. Significantly, they did not transfer the lands to the tillers and kept their hold on lands, forests, and other natural resources.

Before the organisations' commencement, most of the *adivasis* were dependent on agricultural labour, grass-cutting, agri-horticulture, forest, fisheries, and small industries like brick-kilns. Cultivation was dependent on rainfall and they used traditional seeds. Very few *adivasis* cultivated a second crop in the form of pulses and vegetables. The state government, in spite of the existence of dams and rivers, had not provided irrigation facilities to the *adivasis*. Also, the land holding pattern was very unequal. Most of the *adivasis* were landless and sub-marginal landholders and most of the lands were dry lands of extremely poor quality. Lands were not made fertile like that of non-*adivasis*. No land levelling was carried out and there were no facilities of irrigation at all. Agricultural equipment used was generally primitive compared to other farmers.

Their livelihood sources such as small pieces of land, fishing ponds, and timbers were grabbed on a large scale by the moneylenders through fraudulent means such as giving them liquor or food grains often. "Masters" made *adivasi* lands on their own names and *adivasis* lost their land sources to the moneylenders and others at the prices decided by the landlords. Later, outsiders started land grabbing in that area.

Many *adivasis* were bonded labourers under the domination of upper castes including moneylenders and landlords. Women's exploitation by upper caste men was also rampant. The bonded labourers had to work for their landlords day and night, mostly without cash payment, often only given food grains and a few clothes. Generally, clothing was supplied twice a year. Often, they were not relieved from work even when ill. Their "masters" used to exploit them to the extent possible.

Adivasi women were most oppressed. Women's exploitation was two-fold, one by their husbands and second, by their "masters" (landlords). The landlords considered their tenants' wives and the wives of their married servants as their personal property.[3] Therefore, many *adivasis* became impoverished and displaced. They suffered from poor education levels, especially so in the case of one of the most deprived communities, the Katkari *adivasis*. The areas of their habitat were remote with poor access to the outside world and inadequate communication mechanisms.

The law against bonded labour, when implemented, was done so only to the extent of releasing the labourers, but the government did not take appropriate action against persons who violated the law, nor was proper rehabilitation of *adivasis* carried out. Half-hearted implementation efforts of the bonded labour law made *adivasis* unable to stand on their own feet. Many bonded labourers did not receive the government's help or assistance in any form. Thus, their condition worsened. Many began to work in brick-kilns and migrated to other places in search of employment.

On account of the proximity to Mumbai and adjoining industrial areas where construction activities are numerous, Vasai, Bhiwandi, and Wada talukas in Thane district are the areas where brick-kilns are set up. Brick-kilns operate seasonally and are set up each year in the months of November or December, just after the festival of Diwali. For these months, *mukadams* (contractors) identify labourers and pay them money in advance. This also happens to be the lean agricultural season and is thus witness to a large influx of *adivasi* labourers from the adjoining as well as far-flung blocks of Thane, Raigad, and Nashik districts. Builders and brick-kilns settlers get cheap labourers, along with their children, which, in the past, led to the practice of child labour. **Labourers did not receive the minimum wages in spite of the government legislations.** It has been estimated that in the year 2005 there were at least 25,000 *adivasi* migrant child labourers in the brick-kilns of Thane district alone.[4] The children would start working on brick-kilns as early as ages of 4 to 4 years. The practice involved children working from early morning till late night, preparing the mud, carrying bricks and coals, and taking care of younger siblings. Since they spent almost 6 months working, it resulted in dropout from the school. Dropping out of school was a serious problem among the *adivasis*.

The following section is devoted to the condition of the village and its inhabitants before the intervention of organisations.

3. Background of the Respondents Before Joining the Organisations

The following data are based on both the district census handbook, 1981, and an interaction with senior activist members and villagers. It was observed that the amenities such as education, medical, drinking water, post, telegraph, market and communication were poor during the 1980s. The village Tilher selected for the study is in a remote area. In the 1980s, the population of the village was 1959 with 365 households. The population of Scheduled Tribes was 1685.[5] Out of the total population, literates were 223 male and 51 female, i.e. 16%. Almost 50% of the people were non-workers as recorded in the census of 1981.

There were no irrigation facilities and residents were totally dependent on rainfall. People had to walk a distance of 5 to 10 km to fulfil their basic necessities. There was drinking water shortage mostly in the dry months. Women had to fetch water from a long distance. There are many dams in the district, which supply water to the cities, namely, Mumbai and Thane but locals were denied rights to water. Multinational companies, industries, and other businesses received adequate water for their requirements but *adivasis* were neglected by the government. Due to the pumping up of groundwater by soft-drink companies in the area, the water table has gone down and so wells dry up immediately in the summer.

Medical facilities were not available in the village and going to the town for medical health was needed. However, most of them preferred to go to the local *Bhagat* (witch doctor). Superstition was widespread. *Bhagat* and *Bhutali* (witch doctors) were the only medical practitioners they frequented.

Though the Bonded Labourers Abolition Act, 1976, existed,

the practice still continued especially in the Vasai taluka. As mentioned above, residents were part and parcel of the vicious circle of poverty and collective slavery. Vasai taluka was characterised by exploitation by landlords, moneylenders, traders, and gang robbers. Before joining the organisation, they were confined in occupations such as bonded labour, farm labour, manual labour in brick-kilns and mines, landless labour, small farming, and daily wages on truck. They struggled for livelihood, and dignity to live as human beings.

On account of the lack of food availability, they were malnourished. They subsisted on *kadukand* (bitter tuber), *nachani* and *ambil* (red millet and porridge of millet with tamarind). Malnutrition and hunger was common to all. Malnutrition and unsanitary living conditions gave rise to malaria, diarrhoea, and dysentery on a large scale. Additionally, they were addicted to country liquor adding to their health issues.

Their living condition was truly pitiable compared to non-*adivasis*. They lived in abject poverty and in bad debts. Their children wore knickers-sized clothes, and were almost half-clad.

They lived in huts made of *Karvi* (a kind of cane) and thatched with mud and cow dung. In short, they had to live in a sub-human condition. For the political leaders, they were a vote bank, and there was no bargaining capacity among the *adivasis*. There was no support from the government to implement the constitutional provisions for their welfare.

Social interactions with other communities were limited. *Adivasis* did not dare to interact with government officials either. If they spotted police or teachers, they would run away. Social interaction with non-*adivasis* was not accepted. The practices of child labour and child marriage were prevalent and the government machinery was not keen to act against it.

Regarding government facilities, *adivasis* were unaware of these. There were schemes for the welfare of the *adivasis* but such schemes remained on paper owing to non-implementation. They did not have any kind of identity proof such as a certificate of tribe, a ration card, document of 7/12 extract of the land record, or a residence proof. Having no identity cards (ration cards), they were denied benefits of government-initiated development schemes.

It was only after joining the organisations that their socio-economic condition started improving. This is described in the following part.

4. Profile of the Respondents after Joining the Organisations

Primary data were collected on the basis of in-depth interviews with members of the Shramjeevi Sanghatana in the village Tilher of Vasai taluka in Thane district. The author interviewed 70 members and activists of the Shramjeevi Sanghatana who were associated with the Sanghatana since the previous 10 to 15 years.

The sampled village comprises eight hamlets, viz. Varthapada, Tilher, Jadhavpada, Kuwarpada, Khairpada, Palipada, Buradpada and Dhumalpadaas shown in Table 3.1. The hamlets have a Group Gram Panchayat. The distance between *padas* is within two-three kilometres. All the respondents belong to the Scheduled Tribe category. This village is on the Vasai–Bhivandi road.

Table 3.1: Distribution of the Sample Households

Sr. No.	*Name of the Pada*	*Number*	*Per cent*
1.	Varthapada	12	17.2
2.	Tilher	6	8.6
3.	Jadhavpada	15	21.4
4.	Kuwarpada	24	34.3
5.	Khairpada	5	7.1
6.	Palipada	4	5.7
7.	Burudpada	1	1.4
8.	Dhumalpada	3	4.3
	Total	70	100.0

4.1 Social Background of the Respondents

The following section illustrates the respondents' profile, which includes their characteristics such as age, sub-tribe, educational status, etc. The age-wise distribution of the sample households is given in Table 3.2.

The majority (i.e. 65.8%) of the respondents were middle-aged between 31 and 50 years of age. They became part of the organisations since their inception. Of the 70 respondents members, 16 (i.e. 22.86%) were women. In spite of their busy schedule, they gave enough time to share their insights and experiences after joining the Sanghatana.

Table 3.2: Age-wise Distribution of the Respondents

Sr. No.	*Age*	*Number*	*Per cent*
1.	20-30	10	14.2
2.	31-40	23	32.9
3.	41-50	23	32.9
4.	51-60	9	13.9
5.	61-70	5	7.1
Total		70	100

A majority (64%) of the respondents belonged to nuclear families and the remaining 36% respondents were from joint families. This indicates the disintegrating trend of joint families with a movement towards the nuclear family pattern. Almost 97% members were married and very few of them were widows or widowers. Thane district has different kinds of *adivasis* but we interviewed only those who were members of the organisations. The *Warlis* accounted for more than 57.1% of the sample. It was found that they speak in their own mother tongue but more than 74.3% of them also speak Marathi, the state language.

Table 3.3 exhibits the tribe-wise breakup of the respondents. The author interacted with the respondents from Warli, Malhar Koli, Ma Thakur, and Katkari communities in the study village. A majority (57%) of the respondents were Warli followed by Malhar Koli (28.6%). Their hamlets were close to the main village as compared to other communities' hamlets. It was observed that the locality of the Katkaris was furthest away from the main village.

Table 3.3: Tribe-wise Classification of the Respondents

Sr.No.	*Tribe*	*Number*	*Per cent*
1.	Warli	40	57.1
2.	Malhar Koli	20	28.6
3.	Ma Thakur	6	8.6
4.	Katkari	4	5.7
	Total	70	100.0

Table 3.4 focuses on the educational background of the respondents. The importance of education as one of the determining factors of change in any society is well recognised. The literacy level among the *adivasis* was very low compared to non-*adivasis*. It was observed that as many as 72.9% respondents were illiterate but the current generation realised the importance of education. Compared to the literacy level in 1981 (i.e. 16%), there was an increase in literacy levels to about 47.1%. It was observed that in the new generation, there was a greater awareness about the importance of education though their parental generation was illiterate. Earlier, the children of the respondents, who were engaged in brick-kilns, would assist in the jobs of their parents, carrying out tasks like *Balgi* (care taker of their siblings) and *Gawari* (cowherd or shepherd) before the intervention of the educational programme of organisations. After intervention all the members children regularly attend school. Some of the members' sons had completed graduation and some had become teachers in primary schools.

Table 3.4: Educational Background of the Respondents

Sr. No.	*Educational Background*	*Number*	*Per cent*
1.	Illiterate	51	72.9
2.	Second	8	11.4
3.	Fourth	7	10.0
4.	Seventh	1	1.4
5.	SSC	3	4.3
	Total	70	100.0

The drop-out rate is observed to be high in remote areas, especially in the *adivasi* belt, but owing to the efforts of the organisations, it has been reduced considerably. The attitude of respondents' families towards education has changed and they have realised its importance.

The following section addresses how the involvement of respondents in the organisations has increased

4.2 People's Membership and Participation in the Sanghatana

The membership of the Shramjeevi Sanghatana has increased with changing situations. Initially the number of members was just a few hundred but it was over 22,000 in 2007. It is necessary to know the reasons for respondents joining the Sanghatana.

Table 3.5 gives the details of the reasons for joining the Sanghatana. Most of the members joined the Sanghatana owing to the motivation of founder members, Vivek and Vidyutllata Pandit, known as Bhau and Tai, respectively. More than 50% of the members had joined 15 to 20 years ago. The primary reason for joining was for regularisation of land. Thus over 75% of members cited this reason for joining the Sanghatana. The strength of the Sanghatana increased as it began taking up challenging issues.

Table 3.5: Reasons for Joining the Sanghatana by the Respondents

Sr. No.	*Reasons*	*Number*	*Per cent*
1.	To organise	5	7.1
2.	To build strength	2	2.9
3.	For some benefits	7	10.0
4.	To regularise land	53	75.7
5.	To be free from bondage	1	1.4
6.	To assert our rights	2	2.9
	Total	70	100.0

Some members joined the Sanghatana during the village Depiwali's bonded labourers' release programme. Depiwali village is close to Tilher. Members expressed the view that after joining the Shramjeevi Sanghatana, they felt empowered and fearless. Here is the story of *Shantabai Sadanand Samosa* who received help and became a member of the Sanghatana.

> Shantabai was brutally beaten and tortured by her first husband but coincidentally she got introduced to the founder members and received help in preventing this ill treatment. Over a period of time, she became an activist and got involved in the struggles of the Shramjeevi Sanghatana. At present, she owns her home. She has also taken some educational initiatives and helped to make the government machinery accountable. She runs a Balwadi in Tilher and currently assists self-help groups in the village. She has obtained skills of nursing and helps medical caretakers (*Pada Aarogaya Rakshak*).

Here is an example of the Shramjeevi Sanghatana's collective struggle for reclaiming the rights of *adivasis* over natural resources, particularly the forestlands for the livelihood.

> Many *adivasis* have been engaged in forest lands activities and practice farming for many generations, but, due to the eviction order dated 3 May 2002 by the Ministry of Forest and Environment, Government of India, it became necessary for the *adivasis* to get organised and fight against the government's oppression. They carried out a protest in front of the Collector Office of Thane district. The Shramjeevi Sanghatana organised village-level meetings and agitations in blocks and awakened residents about their rights. They also demanded a joint enquiry through the Village Panchayats and a Review Committee for the process of regularisation of *adivasis* lands. Eventually, they got the possession of land along with land entitlements in almost 8 blocks of Thane district. The continued follow-up of Shramjeevi Sanghatana with the state and central government resulted in the issuing of the Resolution by the Ministry of Forest, Government of Maharashtra. This resolution states that crops must not be vandalised, and *adivasis* must not be evicted from their lands, and houses. A large number of similar cases were identified in the Bhiwandi and Vasai blocks. The Ministry of Forest and Environment, Government of India, had asked for the status report of the lands in Maharashtra. Following this, the Government of Maharashtra set up committees to find out the details. With the help of the Gram Sabha, the Forest Village Committee, and the Review Committee the Government of Maharashtra enquired about the cases and gave the Ministry of Forest and Environment, Government of India, a status report of the eligible and the ineligible. The members and activists of Shramjeevi Sanghatana were in the decision-making process, and not just beneficiaries. They were successful in reclaiming 1427 acres of land only in Vasai block during the year 2003.[6]

With this backdrop, the Government of India passed an act called the Scheduled Tribes and Other Traditional Forest Dwellers (Recognition of Forest Rights) Act, 2006, which gives the rights to *adivasis*, nomadic communities, and other forest dwellers. According to the Act, every family would get 10 acres of land once the rules were passed by the government. The rules were ready from January 2008 onwards, and the process of regularisation of lands took place all over.

Almost 60% of the members shared that another motivating factor for becoming a member of the Sanghatana was national celebrations such as Independence Day and Republic Day (an activity mostly appreciated by the members).

It was observed that the members were disciplined. They participated in all the Sanghatana (Shramjeevi Sanghatana) and Sanstha's (Vidhayak Sansad) programmes. More than 92% of the members had a feeling of fearlessness and were confident.

4.3 Capacity-Building Programme

Capacity building of the members is the most important programme run by the organisations and comprises providing perspective and developing skills of its members. It involves imparting knowledge and building confidence while making people aware of their rights. The organisation believes that when oppressed groups become aware of their rights and organise themselves for collective action, they succeed. The activists used various tactics to organise people. These included meetings and camps, press conferences, morchas, appeals to the concerned through press, and writ petitions regarding the bonded labour release and rehabilitation and child labourers in Thane district to the Supreme Court.

Table 3.6: Training by Sanghatana, Sanstha* and Government to the Respondents

Sr. No.	*Type of Organisation*	*Number*	*Per cent*
1.	Training by Sanghatana and Sanstha	43	61.4
2.	Training by Government	15	21.4
3.	Not Applicable	12	17.2
	Total	70	100.0

* Note: Sanstha means Vidhayak Sansad and Sanghatana means Shramjeevi Sanghatana.

The Vidhayak Sansad and Shramjeevi Sanghatana use different methodologies for training members. A special training programme was organised by the organisations for their members six times a year. Various levels of trainers' groups at Usgaon headquarters were formed. Members were given training in human rights, Constitution, Indian Penal Code, and administrative, judiciary, and legislative systems. More than 95% of the members had received training in organising programmes and mobilising people. Table 3.6 reveals that more than 65% of the members benefited from the Sanghatana's training.

The Vidhayak Sansad conducts an innovative training programme for *adivasi* youth and students that has a duration of almost two months. In order to develop leadership qualities among the *adivasi* youths, they are given opportunities and support to contest elections at different levels.

Owing to such concerted capacity-building activities, at the time when the study was conducted in 2006, the Sanstha had its members as people's representatives in 45 Gram Panchayats in 5 talukas. Both the *Sarpanch* and Deputy *Sarpanch* from the study village were members of the Shramjeevi Sanghatana. On account of their organising and mobilising skills, they were able to assert their rights and could build pressure on the concerned departments.

The government also conducts a few training programmes but these are sporadic efforts to train *adivasis* and are restricted to the elected members of the Village Panchayat. Only 20% of the members benefited from the government's training programme. The government focuses on issues-related trainings such as land, forest, agriculture, exploitation, secularism, science, and so on.

The Sanghatana on the other hand, has created an environment where *adivasis* are able to assert their human rights and socio-economic, political, and cultural rights. Every training programme begins with the objective to develop the understanding of Fundamental Rights, followed by issue-based policies, acts, and government resolutions, etc. These training modules particularly the education modules are used in other regions of the state as well.

4.4 Development Initiatives

The focus of the study was to examine the impact of development initiatives by the Vidhayak Sansad and Shramjeevi Sanghatana on the lives of *adivasis*. Here is a list of some of the programmes.

Table 3.7 gives information about the development programmes and its benefits. From among the different programmes of the organisations, a very successful programme was the agriculture and watershed development programme, as shared by the members. With the help of the Sanstha, members received training on farming and additional business. They also received diesel pumps. More than 85% of the members benefited from the watershed development programmes.

Fodder collection was another important programme initiated by the organisations to prevent exploitation by contractors and middlemen. Members pointed out that by collecting fodder and directly selling it in the market, they could earn almost double the amount compared to previous instances when middlemen were involved. The practice enhanced their confidence and challenged middlemen and contractors. About 70% of the members reported participating in fodder collection and distribution during the season. More than 95% members had been a part of organising and mobilising people on human rights, legal aid support, and educational and political support of the processes. The grain bank is another major activity reported by the members.

Table 3.7: Benefits of Organisations' Programmes

Sr. No.	*Programme*	*Number*	*Per cent*
1.	Grain Bank	28	40.0
2.	Brick Kiln Industry	37	52.9
3.	Fodder Collection	50	71.4
4.	Diesel Pump	60	85.7
5.	Watershed Programme	61	87.1
6.	Police Legal Information	66	94.3
7.	Political Awareness	67	95.7
8.	Employment Awareness	67	95.7
9.	Organising and Mobilising	69	98.6
10.	Educational Awareness	69	98.6
11.	Health Awareness	69	98.6
12.	Women and Child Awareness	69	98.6

Health awareness has also considerably increased among members. Approximately all the members had participated in health, women and child development programmes, and the employment guarantee scheme. These programmes helped in building women's strength through the Self Help Groups (SHGs). One of the very popular programmes for women's empowerment is known as *Thingi* (a spark). Through the *Thingi* programme, promotion of SHGs was carried out. An interesting example is as follows:

> A large number of women from Mandvi village started home-based small-scale businesses like grinding spices. The Savitribai Phule *Bachat Gat* (saving group) obtained a weekly marker tender and started a multi-business. This helped in instilling confidence among the women members. The group grew vegetables to earn income. Prior to such income-generation initiatives, women's work was considered to be meaningless but after such efforts, women's work began to be considered as valuable. Some of the members from the women's group put forth the idea of purchasing a tractor and also managed to get a loan for it. They used it for multiple activities like transporting vegetables, sand, and stones. For the first time, in the history *adivasis,* women mustered the courage to purchase a tractor and proved that they were not subordinate, and could become socio-economically independent if given the opportunity. Such is the beginning of empowerment of women in any society.

The benefits of joining the Sanghatana were quite visible. The author observed the benefits of agricultural aid received from the Vidhayak Sansad and Shramjeevi Sanghatana.

Almost 94% of the members had received agricultural aid from the Vidhayak Sansad and Shramjeevi Sanghatana. Earlier, they had to take loans for consumption to fulfil social and religious requirements, and mostly to meet the need of agricultural equipment. With agricultural aid, loans were no longer needed to meet the family needs or agricultural needs.

> This story of Keshav Nankar pertains to the agricultural programmes. As a boy, he and his entire family fell into bondage for a small loan taken by his father. Keshav wanted to go to school but could not because his "master" wanted him to tend to the cattle. Later, after his marriage, both Keshav and his wife were in bondage. They worked for over 16 hours a day. In return, they received some food (bread or rice). They were abused and at times even starved. With motivation from founder members of the Shramjeevi Sanghatana, Keshav became a member of the

> organisation. As a member, he received training in many areas, but his main interest was pursuing agriculture. The Shramjeevi Sanghatana founder members provided him space and opportunities for research in agro-based programmes. Since the organisation has its centre for agricultural development for the rehabilitation of the released bonded labourers in the study area, he received assistance and began to support other released bonded labourers. He was in fact the first released bonded labour of the Shramjeevi Sanghatana. It was 25 years ago, that Keshav, through the efforts of the union, escaped from the horrors of his bonded labour.

The Shramjeevi Sanghatana received the Anti-Slavery International Award in 1999 and the first freed bonded labourer (Keshav) attended the award ceremony in London. Now, Keshav is a symbol of the resilience of the human spirit and a role model for others. He serves as a Chairman of the Shramjeevi Sanghatana and is the head of the agriculture department. Keshav has helped more than 6,000 bonded labourers to gain their freedom. The Sanghatana members appreciated his courage and commitment to the *adivasi* people. He formed the freed bonded labourers' collective farming in various villages to grow watermelons and vegetables in large quantities. Through the organisation, initial agricultural support such as diesel pumps for lift irrigation, seeds and fertilisers, are provided. Today, Keshav is involved in agricultural experiments in various villages. Owing to his initiatives, kitchen gardens and collective farming projects have improved. His dream is to grow export quality vegetables and export them to other countries. He has also developed various techniques to understand subordination and poverty in the *adivasi* community."

4.5 Benefits of the Development Schemes

The implementation of government schemes always remained poor in remote areas but due to the awareness and pressure of the Sanghatana, people benefited from the government schemes. A significant interim order of the Supreme Court dated November 28, 2001 issued a directive to the Union and state governments to implement the eight food-related schemes fully as per official guidelines (see Table 3.8). It is the responsibility of the state government to ensure that there is proper implementation of the schemes, which are meant for the socio-economically marginalised people.

Table 3.8 provides information about several tribal development schemes such as education, food security, old-age pensions, child and women's development, and maternity benefits. More than 60% of the members benefited from the government schemes. Nearly 60% of the children received educational benefits.

Table 3.8: Benefits from Government's Schemes

Sr. No.	*Schemes*	*Number*	*Per cent*
1.	Indira Awas Scheme	14	20.0
2.	Maternity Benefits	30	42.9
3.	Tribal Sub-Plan (TSP) Hostel Benefit	42	60.0
4.	Tribal Sub-Plan (TSP) Benefit	43	61.4
5.	Women and Child Development	44	62.9
6.	Food for Work	62	88.6
7.	Awareness of Family Planning	66	94.3
8.	EGS Benefit	68	97.1

The right to work was made a fundamental right in 1977, when the Government of Maharashtra provided it through its Employment Guarantee Act. The prime slogan of this scheme is 'Work for all' and the scheme has helped many in obtaining employment, especially in the lean period.

The right to work was implemented through the Employment Guarantee Scheme (EGS) in the study area as well. Nearly 97% of the families benefited from the EGS. Its impact is seen in the reduction of the seasonal migration of *adivasis*.

In order to reduce the malnutrition and anaemia among the *adivasi* children and women, the government initiated schemes like food security through the maternity benefits to the pregnant women. It was observed that all members had become health conscious. In the case of family planning too, the level of awareness was quite high. As far as the maternity benefit scheme is concerned, the benefits derived by members have been somewhat less compared to other benefits. This implies that there are many programmes and schemes meant for the development of *adivasi*s but not all of them are implemented fully. The activists of Sanghatana reported that effective implementation of the government schemes occurred to a large extent after members were aware about the schemes and pro-actively began asking for their implementation. The members of the two organisations, Vidhayak Sansad and Shramjeevi Sanghatana used innovative actions for ensuring implementation of government schemes. Activists had cordial relations with government servants and used this to exert pressure on them. The Sanghatana built up awareness about government programmes regarding rights already granted to labourers through peaceful protests and by creating public opinion through media and mass based programmes.

However, the Sanghatana is an issue-based organisation and used schemes such as EGS as a tool to help the community understand the concept of the right to work. In the year they held an awareness campaign for employment rights in all blocks of the Shramjeevi Sanghatana. By organising a cycle rally, they identified work sites and helped in preparation of application filing and getting job cards. In Vasai taluka, the Sanghatana was able to obtain more than 2,000 job cards not only for its members but also for non-members. In all talukas, they were able to obtain almost 20,000 applications and job cards.[7] They trained the poor to believe in their freedom, dignity, self-esteem, self-reliance, and gender equality. People's involvement in the Shramjeevi Sanghatana helped them to obtain the benefits of the government and organisations' schemes. The following data pertains to the economic condition of the respondents.

4.6 Economic Condition of the Respondents

Economic status describes the various factors of property holding by the respondents that include house, lands, income, and so on. Table 3.9 describes the condition of the house with its relation to ownership, entitlement, number of rooms and amenities such as sanitation and electricity. The author has observed three types of housing such as Kuchha, Semi-Pucca and Pucca. Kuchha houses are made of Karvi grass (ken type of grass) with thatched roof, Semi-Pucca houses are made of mud with bricks and ken grass roof, and Pucca houses are made of cement concrete.

Table 3.9: Type of the House of the Respondents

Sr. No.	*Type*	*Number*	*Per cent*
1.	Kuchha	14	20.0
2.	Semi-Pucca	25	35.7
3.	Pucca	31	44.3
	Total	70	100.0

Having their own home was the dream of many *adivasis*. A large majority i.e. 98%) of the householder had permanent houses and only 2% lived in rented houses. A majority (i.e. 88.6%) of the respondents had two-room tenements with a kitchen and a cowshed. The members observed that having their own house was considered a great achievement in their life.

In Indian society, women have to struggle for equal property rights, but in the *adivasi* community this is not a problem. Some 20% of the women had their names on the property records. Most no longer migrated to other places because of their permanent dwellings. Earlier they would migrate to Surat, Ahmedabad, Baroda, and Mumbai for a period of six months every year.

Some 42% of the families had sanitation facilities in the village. Sanitation includes toilets and bathrooms. Access and availability is a major challenge, especially in remote areas. As many as 92% of the families in all hamlets of Tilher village had electricity All the respondents had adequate water availability in their own hamlets. The Sanghatana members as well as members of the Gram Panchayat take care of drinking water.

Table 3.10 focuses on holdings of domestic animals by the respondents. More than 60% families owned chicken and oxen. Many of them also owned other animals like cows, buffaloes, and goats. They tended to own a large number of chickens. Although previously rearing chickens and goats, at that time they were compelled to give them to forest officials but this was no longer the case now. Almost 68.6% of the families owned chickens for their livelihood purpose. About 62.9% of the families owned oxen for their agricultural and transport purposes.

Table 3.10: Domestic Animals of the Respondents

Sr. No.	*Animals*	*Number*	*Per cent*
1.	Chickens	48	68.6
2.	Oxen	44	62.9

Table 3.11 reveals that respondents owned assets and possessions such as bullock-carts, bicycles, motorcycles, televisions, mobiles, and auto rickshaws. The needs of *adivasis* are very limited and they are happy with few possessions. Traditionally they tend to rely on natural resources for their survival and livelihood but in the changing scenario, they are moving towards modernity. The author assessed holding, including electronic appliances and agricultural equipment. It was seen that 55.7% of the families owned bullock-carts, crucial in agricultural activities. About 57.1% of the respondents owned bicycles. Around 35.7% of the families owned tape-recorders and radios as a source of entertainment. It was observed that 28.6% of the respondents had television sets and some of them also had a CD player. Many of the respondents owned mobiles and motorcycles as well.

Table 3.11: Housing Assets and Possessions

Sr. No.	*Type*	*Number*	*Per cent*
1.	Bullock-Carts	39	55.7
2.	Bicycles	40	57.1
3.	Tape-Radios	25	35.7
4.	Televisions	20	28.6
5.	Motorcycles	13	18.6
6.	Mobiles	28	40.0
7.	Auto Rickshaws	4	5.7

The ration card is one of the important evidences required for the benefits of government schemes. Previously, respondents had not been given ration cards and hence were not eligible for the benefits of any scheme. After the intervention of the organisations, nearly 94% of the respondents possessed yellow cards (indicating their Below Poverty Line status). They were now eligible for the benefits of the government schemes. Further, their income levels also increased.

Occupation or economic activity of the people is an indicator of their economic status. Table 3.12 gives data about members' occupations.

Table 3.12: Additional Occupations of the Respondents

Sr. No.	*Additional Occupation*	*Number*	*Per cent*
1.	Animal husbandry	2	2.9
2.	Vegetable growing	17	24.3
3.	Brick making	9	12.9
4.	Firewood collection	2	2.9
5.	Wage earning	1	1.4
6.	Self-employment	1	1.4
7.	Not applicable	38	54.2
	Total	70	100.0

In the case of the previous generation, as many as 84% of the families were dependent on others' farms, but the present pattern of livelihood showed that only 24% were labourers, and a large majority comprising 75% cultivated their own lands. This was a significant change in their livelihood pattern. Many families were also engaged in other occupations like animal husbandry, growing and selling vegetables, *Warli* paintings, basket making and some other self-employed activities. For a few years, members did collective farming and cultivated watermelons. Both women and men before, they were engaged in both agricultural and non-agricultural activities. At the time of the survey, many of the members had their own kitchen gardens to fulfil their daily vegetable needs.

Earlier *adivasis* had to migrate for their livelihood. They had no secure sources of food grains too. Women and children were the most vulnerable amongst *adivasis*. Additionally, the rampant exploitation by their "masters" resulted in poor health. Migration had caused malnutrition and there had been many hunger deaths in the district. Now, almost 78% of the families had ceased to migrate for employment but there were some 20% of the members who continued to do so.

Land is the prime source of livelihood and status for many in villages of India. But, for *adivasis*, it is the only means of survival. A large number of *adivasis* survive on a small-land-holding on which paddy and *nagali* (red millet) are grown.

Table 3.13 provides data on land holding by members (after joining the organisations). It was observed that almost 66 of the 70 members now held lands. The few landless members were dependent on wage earning in the form of rice during the harvesting season.

Tribals have reclaimed their forest land encroached upon by the forest department and use it for their livelihood purposes. A few owned ancestral land. There has been a wide range of land holding pattern from landless, marginal to medium. There were 63% of the members who now had small and medium land holdings.

Table 3.13: Size of Land Holdings of the Respondents

Sr. No.	*Size*	*Number*	*Per cent*
1	Landless	4	5.7
2	Marginal Farmers (less than 1 HA.)	22	31.4
2	Small Farmers (1.0 to 2.0 HA.)	35	50.0
3	Medium Farmers (4.0 to 10.0 HA.)	9	12.9
	Total	70	100.0

All the members grew paddy as a major crop and a few members took up a second crop (Rabi crop) such as pulses and vegetables. More than 60% of the members were involved in taking first seasonal (Kharif crop) crops.

Table 3.14 gives the crop yield in quintals. The crop cultivated is mostly rice. It was observed that the members had agricultural yield ranging from 2 to 16 quintals (this is calculated in *Mann* which is equal to 20 kg). More than 75% of the members had an annual yield ranging between 6 and 12 quintals. A few member respondents reported a yield of 16 quintals of paddy.

They also grew oilseeds, wheat, and a few varieties of pulses. Thus, it was clear that they now had sufficient food grain availability for the whole year. Many of them were happy with their earnings. More than 80% of the members said they were not worried about their annual food security. Before the intervention of organisations they had to spend their day and night for food gathering and doing the rotation kind of farming, but now, they had maintainable earnings. They sometimes used the high yielding varieties (HYV) seeds such as hybrid rice, vegetables, and fruits in farming for a better yield.

Table 3.14: Agricultural Income of the Respondents

Sr. No.	Rice Yield in Quintal	Number	Per cent
1.	Two	6	8.6
2.	Four	7	10.0
3.	Six	18	25.7
4.	Eight	16	22.9
5.	Ten	9	12.9
6.	Twelve	9	12.9
7.	Fourteen	1	1.4
8.	Sixteen	4	5.7
	Total	70	100.0

They claimed 29 acres land from the *Sawkar* (moneylender) in the village *Sawkar* and Kaner. They reclaimed 75 acres land from Mafia in the village Poman with the help of organisations. These claims exerted pressure on moneylenders who started giving *adivasis'* lands back. A respondent revealed his experience of success in getting his land back.

> Fifty-five-year-old Mr. Aatamaram Lahu Renjad who lives in Tilher is illiterate. He wanted to study but could not study because of poverty. He spent his childhood as a bonded labourer at a *Patil's* home. Almost 25 years ago, he was a tenant cultivating 5 acres of land. A couple of years later, the "master" tried to sell that land because the "master" knew that taking the land back was not possible for him. At the same time, coincidentally, the bonded labourers' release programme was taking place in the village Depiwali (a landmark village in the struggle of bonded labourers' release). Renjad interacted with the founder members of the Shramjeevi Sanghatana and shared his story with the members. He then became a member and participated in various orientation programmes conducted by the organisations. He received training pertaining to the information about human rights. He also obtained agriculture-related skills with the help of the Vidhayak Sansad and Shramjeevi Sanghatana. Meanwhile, he received help from government offices to reclaim the land. After a long struggle against the *"master"*, he claimed 5 acres of land. It was the biggest victory in the history of the Renjad family. At the time of the survey, he owned 10 acres of land (as per land records) and obtained a high yield per annum approximately 50-quintal paddy. He had his own house, irrigation facility, and agricultural

equipment. He was able to provide quality education to his children. He got elected to his village Gram Panchayat. At the time of the survey, his son had become the Deputy *Sarpanch* of Tilher.

In Indian society, women are not considered for holding assets, particularly land and houses. Having any kind of asset is an empowerment and status symbol in society. However, due to the deliberate efforts of civil society organisations, women obtained equal property rights. Close to 30% of women now held their land *patta* in their names.

The case of Burudpada signifies an important struggle for reclaiming of land of *adivasis* from "masters". According to the Land Tenancy Act, 1960, 32-G, tenants can claim the cultivating land (land to the tiller). Therefore, the activists and members fought against the owners and got almost 35 acres land back for the *adivasi* family. The members of the Burud family cultivated that land since their childhood but every year their owner used to take 75% of food grains. With the help of 25 members and activists of the Shramjeevi Sanghatana, the land was reclaimed. This happened in 1998 in Tilher.

The above-mentioned two cases also reported the highest paddy yield in the village and among the members of the Shramjeevi Sanghatana. Respondents shared that prior to intervention of the organisations, they could not fulfil the minimum requirement of two square meals a day, but they now had 50-60 quintals yield per annum. They had become secure with respect to their food requirement and they were able to sell a portion of it in the market. Thus, more than 80% of the respondents now had food sufficiency. Similarly, access and entitlement to land had increased more than 94%. Income of any family is the means for leading a fulfilling requirement such as food security, education, and health. Traditionally, in *adivasi* communities, it was difficult to obtain employment. They engaged in food gathering and many were bonded.

Table 3.15 reveals the families' monthly income. More than 40% of the respondents had Rs. 1,500 as monthly income from the sources of land wages, etc. Owing to the reduction in migration, they had stability, and due to the established relations between the employer and employee, they now received rightful wages.

Table 3.15: Monthly Income of the Respondents' Families

Sr. No.	*Income (in rupees)*	*Number*	*Per cent*
1.	1000	17	24.3
2.	1500	31	44.3
3.	2000	11	15.8
4.	2500	5	7.1
5.	3000	5	7.1
6.	3500	1	1.4
	Total	70	100.0

Previously exploitation by landlords, moneylenders, brick-kiln owners, and such others was rampant but with the intervention of organisations, this was almost eliminated. Having increased their income levels, they now deposited their savings in local banks and were able to educate their children.

Table 3.16 gives the details of the families' monthly income in rupees hamlet-wise. The monthly income was calculated considering income from the wages and yield of crops. In each family, some members used to work on others' farms or government-supported employment programmes and thus they had additional sources of income.

Table 3.16: Hamlet-wise Monthly Income of the Respondents' Families

		Monthly Income in Rupees						
Sr. No.	*Hamlet*	*1000*	*1500*	*2000*	*2500*	*3000*	*3500*	*Total*
1.	Varthapada	4	2	1	2	3		12
2.	Tilher		2	4				6
3.	Jadhavpada	3	9		2		1	15
4.	Kuwarpada	8	13	1	1	1		24
5.	Khairpada	1	4					5
6.	Palipada		1	3				4
7.	Burudpada					1		1
8.	Dhumalpada	1		2				3
	Total	17	31	11	5	5	1	70

Out of 70 members, 59 families had a monthly income ranging between Rs. 1,000 and Rs. 2,000, which was in contrast to earlier times when they used to be in debt to moneylenders and landlords. A majority of the members from Kuwarpada reported high earnings with some of the families reporting more than Rs. 3,000 monthly income.

Even these reported incomes earned in rupees and having their own saving account was deemed by them to be a major achievement in their lives. The data exhibit that the older members of the organisations had better income levels (these were from Kuwarpada and Jadhavpada hamlets).

Table 3.17: Tribe-wise Respondents' Families Income

		Monthly Income of the Respondents in Rupees						
Sr. No.	*Tribe*	*1000*	*1500*	*2000*	*2500*	*3000*	*3500*	*Total*
1.	Warli	12	15	5	3	5		40
2.	Malhar Koli	3	11	4	2			20
3.	Ma Thakur	2	4					6
4.	Katkari		1	2			1	4
	Total	17	31	11	5	5	1	70

Table 3.17 reveals the families' income tribe-wise. It was observed that the highest numbers of earners were Warlis *adivasis* and the lowest were Katkaris. Still, most *adivasis* tribes were able to earn at least Rs.1,500-2,000 monthly, The *adivasis* have gained confidence in earning as their right to work and right to life with dignity.

Table 3.18: Changing Households' Standard of Living[8]

Sr. No.	*Name of the Hamlet*	*Standard of Living*			*Total*
		*Low**	*Medium***	*High****	
1.	Varthapada	2	8	2	12
2.	Tilher	4	2		6
3.	Jadhavpada	5	10		15
4.	Kuwarpada	4	16	4	24
5.	Khairpada	1	3	1	5
6.	Palipada		4		4
7.	Burudpada			1	1
8.	Dhumalpada	2		1	3
	Total	18	43	9	70

Table 3.18 shows the picture of the standard of living of the households hamlet-wise. One observes that more than 43

respondents were in the medium level. The highest standard of living was reported by respondents from the hamlets of Varthapada, Jadhavpada, and Kuwarpada. Also, it was observed that those reporting high living standards were from the *Warli* community.

Improved standard of living led to improvements in their health, education, food, clothing, housing conditions and has increased ownership of housing assets, land holdings, and electronic and automobile possessions. Thus, the respondents' participation in programmes and benefits of the programmes resulted in improving their socio-economic status. They gained confidence in getting the right wages and equal pay for equal work. There were 18 respondents in low, the highest 43 were in medium and about 9 were in high standard of living categories.

Table 3.19 describes the standard of living status of *adivasis* (Tribes). It was observed that their income levels had increased. It was observed that a majority of the *Warli* tribes benefited because of the organisations' work. All the *Katkari* members reached the medium level. Earlier, they had been left out from developmental programmes but now they had become a part

Table 3.19: Tribe-wise Standard of Living

Sr. No.	*Name of the Tribe*	*Standard of Living*			*Total*
		*Low**	*Medium***	*High****	
1.	Warli	8	24	8	40
2.	Malhar Koli	9	10	1	20
3.	Ma Thakur	1	5		6
4.	Katkari		4		4
	Total	18	43	9	70

* *Low*: Kuchha house (thatched roof hut), Marginal land holdings (less than 1HA.), agricultural income (2-4 quintal) and livestock (2-5 chickens).

** *Medium*: Semi-Pucca house (mud and brick walls and ken roof), small land holdings (1.0 to 2.0 HA.), agricultural income (6-10 quintal), livestock (5-10 chickens and 2-3 oxen), bullock carts and bicycles.

*** *High*: Pucca house (cement concrete), medium land holdings (4.0 to 10.0 HA.), agricultural income (12-16 quintal), livestock (more than 10 chickens, 2-4 oxen, 1-2 cows and 1-2 goats), bullock carts, bicycles, motorcycles, tape-radios, televisions, fans, mobiles and furniture.

of the development process. Their changing socio-economic situation led to a life of dignity wherein they could now be fearless. The following part focuses on changing social relations.

4.7 Social Relations

Social relations and interactions are an important aspect in social transformation in any society. Earlier, social relations were observed to be poor in terms of interactions with other communities. Different *adivsasi* communities were observed to not even share food together, for example the Warli and Katkari did not eat food together or interact with each other. Within the same community also, there were different cultural rituals. The Katkaris were deemed to be subordinate and were treated with less dignity. Though the village had a majority of *adivasi* population, there were many social restrictions on the Katkari and Mathakur *adivasis* but now they had become free from these social restrictions and were now observed to be eating together, fetching water from the same sources, participating in marriages of other communities, and carrying out worship of gods and goddesses. In other words, interactions among different *adivasi* communities had been encouraged.

Owing to the participation in various awareness programmes and benefits of the government and organisation schemes, their income levels increased which helped them to increase their social relations with different communities, and power structures. The standard of living impacted their social relations that included the interactions within and outside the communities, participation in each other's programmes, collective celebrations of traditions and festivals, sharing food together, use of collective water resources and political positioning. The most important aspect was the changed behaviour of shopkeepers, moneylenders and landlords.

Similarly, understanding of *adivasis* about the health and family planning and their realisation of adverse impact of child marriages impacted the practice of arranging marriages. The author observed that more than 75% of the families were aware about the legal age of marriages. Earlier girls were married off immediately after attaining puberty, but this has now changed.

> Here is the case of Mr. Mahadu Dharma Gavit who is a Katkari and lives in Palipada. He is almost 55 years old. He is a member of the Shramjeevi Sanghatana for the last 23 years. Earlier his entire family was engaged in basket making and collection of firewood. It was revealed that they were tortured and beaten brutally by forest officials and always had to provide money and chickens to them and there was unending exploitation. They had no communication with other communities because they were treated as the lowest in the village hierarchy. They had also to carry dead animals. The programme of the release of bonded labourers motivated him and he became a member of the Sanghatana. Now, he has very good relations with others.

At the time the study was conducted, all the members had socio-religious acceptance and shared food together. Previously non-*adivasis* treated *adivasis* as untouchables. Even for their daily needs like sugar, tea, oil, etc, they were not given credit because shopkeepers were not sure of repayment, but, now all the members have access and can get commodities on the basis of credit. This shows a change in the attitudes of non-*adivasis*.

There was now full access to temples, common water sources and there was a friendly feeling amongst all. More than 98% of women had participated in different programmes conducted by the organisations. The author observed that women were always in the forefront in all kinds of protest, training programmes and participate in the decision-making process. Interestingly, 100% of the women went to the weekly market and decided on how to use their money. They now enjoyed equal status in their families.

4.8 Political Achievement

In order to conscientise the members of the Sanghatana, founders organised special training and awareness programmes. The author observed the enhanced status of the members through their participation in local self-governance brought about by improved political awareness. Democratic decentralisation becomes meaningful when it reaches the last person of society in developing their leadership qualities and participation in the decision-making process.

All the members had their names in the voters' list and had

voter cards. Approximately 18% of the members had contested the Gram Panchayat election in 2005 through the panel of the Shramjeevi Sanghatana. Significantly, all the members of the Sanghatana had won the election. Members of the Gram Panchayat were active and one member of the Sanghatana is currently the *Sarpanch* (head of the Village Panchayat) of Tilher. The organisations organise all the Gram Sabhas. More than 35 Gram Panchayats' *Sarpanches* were women and they were members of the Shramjeevi Sanghatana in Thane district. A freed woman bonded labourer had become a member of the Thane Zilla Parishad.

> Ms. Anita Dhangada was born in a bonded family. In 1989, Anita approached the Sanghatana's founder members to seek help and became a member. Immediately, the Sanghatana filed a formal case against the powerful landlord. The landlord had full control over the village and no one dared to complain against him, but with the intervention of the Sanghatana, people from even surrounding villages got together to support Anita. During the case, the landlord stopped giving financial support to Anita's family. With support from the government, activists confronted the landlord and succeeded. The landlord released not only Anita but also her entire family of 22 members. Anita later became interested in politics and fought against mafia politicians and got elected. She was perhaps the first freed bonded woman who was elected as a representative in the district politics. She is respected by all members of the community and local bodies. She is involved in the Public Distribution System and intervened for the rights of neglected people. She helped many people in getting their ration cards. As an elected representative she worked to make school teachers and health workers accountable. There were many complaints and demands for potable water in every school and Balwadis. She immediately commissioned a survey and fulfilled the students' requirements. She has utilised her influence in different departments and got work sanctioned by the Zilla Parishad in building roads, schools, and water and sanitation facilities.

The third chapter pertained to the field investigation and findings and the author focused on describing the past and present conditions of the respondent members of the organisation with the aim of explaining the level of conscientisation of the activists. The next chapter will focus on the impact of conscientisation on the lives of *adivasis*.

NOTES

1. Government of India: *Report of the Commissioner for Scheduled Castes and Scheduled Tribes*, New Delhi, Twenty-ninth Report, 1987-1989.
2. Ibid., p. 121.
3. Saldanha, Indra Munshi: Tribal Women in the Warli Revolt, 1945-1947, *Economic and Political Weekly*, Vol. XXI, No.17, *Review of Women Studies*, April 26, 1986, p. WS-43.
4. Jayachandran, Usha: *Vidhayak Sansad's Bhonga Shalas; Bringing Schools to Tribal Migrant Children–A Case Study*, January 10, 2004.
5. Government of Maharashtra: *Census of India 1981; District Census Handbook Thane*, Government Printing Press, Bombay, 1986.
6. Shramjeevi Sanghatana: *Annual Report 2005*, Usgaon Dongari, Thane, p. 12.
7. The figures shared by the activist of Vasai Taluka during the field visit. It also reflected in the Shramjeevi Sanghatana's annual report 2006.

4

Impact of Rights Based Approach to Development and Advocacy

1. Introduction

In the previous chapter, based on the empirical data, it was observed that the socio-economic condition of the *adivasis* had been changing with the intervention of the Vidhayak Sansad and Shramjeevi Sanghatana. After joining the organisations, there were positive changes also in the cultural and political condition of the members. The processes that led to such changes need to be assessed. Hence, it is important to study mechanisms and innovative ways adopted in conscientisation and in organising and mobilising the *adivasis.*

After the struggle against exploitation, and for human rights and social justice, the organisations pursued the path of development. This chapter assesses the impact-making processes initiated by the organisations. The author interviewed grassroots leaders and had informal meetings with many activists as well as members of the organisations to obtain the necessary information. The author also observed and assessed components administered through various programmes of the Vidhayak Sansad and the Shramjeevi Sanghatana.

As noted previously, the socio-economic condition of the members was pitiable before the intervention of the organisations with no opportunities for orientation and education. This made them incapable of understanding the nature of exploitation or of having the motivation to fight against injustice. However, after the intervention of the organisations, not only did the members benefit but their family members, the community, and the whole village benefited. Conscientisation was an important factor in educating the *adivasis*. The following section focuses on the role of conscientisation and its critical factors that helped raise the consciousness of the *adivasis* with respect to human rights.

2. The Role of Conscientisation in Liberating the *Adivasis* from Bondage

Since the focus of the study is on conscientisation of *adivasis* with the intervention of the Vidhayak Sansad and Shramjeevi Sanghatana, the author used the theoretical framework of conscientisation as an instrument of liberation. According to Freire, the term conscientisation refers to perceiving social, political, and economic contradictions, and taking actions against these oppressive factors of reality. Education of the oppressed/deprived *adivasis* was carried out through orientation, trainings, organising, mobilising, and through developing leadership qualities among the members.

The conscientisation process focused on restoring fundamental rights of the people through organising and mobilising them. The other aspect of this process was providing strong support for skills building through programmes associated with livelihood. Thus, programmes were organised for the orientation of members through the Shramjeevi Sanghatana to enable members to understand the ways of exploitation by the socially and economically powerful landlords, moneylenders, and contractors in the area. Initially, the challenge was to create awareness about the system of bonded labour and mobilise collective action against it. Because of the attitude of moneylenders and landlords, the founders Mr. Vivek Pandit and Mrs. Vidyutllata were not accepted in the villages and were treated as outsiders. However, once the bonded labourers realised that the founders were taking risks to assist with their release and rehabilitation, they began cooperating with them.

It was while working on the issues of health and education in the Vasai block that the founders encountered several cases of bonded labour. There were many reasons for the growth and perpetuation of the bonded labour system, such as extreme poverty, inability to find employment, lack of mobility, not being paid appropriate wages, ignorance, illiteracy, as well as neglect by the state machinery. Exploitation by some in the villages, high expenditure on rituals/birth of children/death/ superstitions were other compounding factors. The Bonded Labour Abolition Act, 1976, existed only on paper and was not implemented in spite of many efforts. However, with the help of the government, the organisations began the process of implementing the Act in Vasai taluka in the year 1982.

The founders identified 8 bonded labourers in the village of Dahisar but the labourers were unwilling to file cases against their creditors or take action against their "masters". The labourers in fact were even unwilling to talk to others and often ran away to end a conversation. After a year-long effort, the labourers were persuaded to file cases against their "masters". The Vidhayak Sansad and Shramjeevi Sanghatana helped release 5 bonded labourers with the help of the Tahsildar on May 12, 1982.[1] This was the first such case of legal release of bonded labourers in the history of Maharashtra and Thane district. During the continued struggle for the release of bonded labourers, the organisations received constant support from the *Sakal* newspaper. The organisations not only helped release the bonded labourers, but also recovered the appropriate compensation from their "masters". In the Virar case, they recovered the sum of Rs. 12,884 by appearing before the Labour Commission of Thane (see Appendix p. 164).[2]

They also succeeded in awakening people to their rights with the help of the Labour Commission. To tackle the challenges and to fight against entrenched power centres, there needs to be a counter power. With this logic, the founders initiated mass mobilisation for strengthening the Shramjeevi Sanghatana in the district. Slogans in the local dialect were designed to mobilise people. The first slogan that was coined was *adivasi dhor nay; manoos hay* (*Adivasis* are not animals, they are human beings). Using this slogan, the activists identified *adivasis* in bondage, and assured to free them. When they gained in confidence, bonded labourers began organising themselves against the "masters". Participatory education helped in making the Sanghatana strong and sustainable.

Another slogan *sosnar nahi aamhi atayachar, aamhi ladhayala hao tayar* (We will not tolerate any kind of injustice, we are equipped to fight) was coined and this slogan became popular all over the taluka. The slogan propelled more *adivasis* to seek assistance from the Vidhayak Sansad and Shramjeevi Sanghatana to liberate their relatives from the "masters". Many of the members from Tilher were part of the process. The local battle against the "masters" was a dangerous task.

The *Shibir* was the main activity organised to help bonded labourers understand issues and to devise strategies to tackle them. These *Shibirs* played an important role in building the strength of unorganised labourers to fight for their rights. Often, members faced attacks from paid goons sent by moneylenders and landlords. Even when beaten up brutally, they followed the principle of non-violence and reacted with people's power and constitutional weapons against it.

Women members were in the forefront in the special drive for the release of bonded labourers. Two such courageous women among the group were Sonibai and Deobai who initiated the process of contacting people and holding collective meetings in the various villages. The group of women initiated the 'labourers release programme' to get the minimum wages and equal wages. During the year 1984, their demand was to get Rs. 7 per day minimum wages as their right but the "masters" were unwilling to pay this amount. To combat this, the women protested through innovative ways, e.g. *bombala Morcha* (shouting agitation) against the "masters". The *bombala Morcha* resulted in the boycott of labourers by their "masters". The boycott continued for 14 days but the *adivasi*s did not relent. As it was the harvest season, the "masters" had to agree to pay minimum wages to the labourers. Such successes built up unity and strength among members and helped in strengthening the Sanghatana.

The team of activists then developed cadres in the blocks. The team of cadres decided to help release their brethren who were still in bondage. The cadres began awareness activities in west Vasai, where they identified a large number of bonded labourers. Activists covered many villages and held village meetings relating to the release of bonded labourers. Speeches during meetings focused on the socio-economic condition of *adivasis* and factors leading to such a condition. *Adivasis* discussed issues relating to their daily needs but were determined that they would not bow down before the landlords. They said *kadu kand khau, kaula khau, belkadaya khau pan malkache pay dharnar naahi* (we will eat bitter roots, crabs and bitter onions but we will not bow down before the landlords).

At the same time, the opposition forces, i.e. "masters" were becoming powerful and stopped providing food rations and work to the labourers to make them more vulnerable. However, the increasing force of the activities of the organisations was a source of strength to members to unite and rebel against the "masters". Meanwhile, the leaders of both the Vidhayak Sansad and Shramjeevi Sanghatana approached the media, government officers, and advocates, and obtained support from other well-wishers in helping release and rehabilitate the labourers. In the second phase, the Shramjeevi Sanghatana helped release as many as 300 bonded labourers in Vasai block (see Appendix pp. 165).

The *adivasis* strengthened their struggle against *Jamindari* with the slogan of *jamindari, bhandvaldari nashta karuya chala ra; gharat basun bhagnar nahi aata rastyvar chala ra* (if we have to destroy the Zamindari and capitalistic systems, then we need to get out of our homes and protest against it at all levels). Songs and slogans of this kind proved powerful for organising *Vethbeegars* against exploitative forces. Slogans motivated collective action. Another important slogan that became popular during the release programme of the bonded labourers was: *aamacha ladha nayasathi; manoos mahnhun jagnyasathi* (our struggle is for justice; our struggle is to live like human beings).

The Government of Maharashtra declared that the system of bonded labour did not exist in the state but in 1984 the Shramjeevi Sanghatana wrote a letter to the Supreme Court of India. The Honorable Justice P.N. Bhagawati treated the letter as a writ petition and ordered an Enquiry Commission by the Supreme Court of India.[3] Dr. Satyaranjan Sathe and Vasudha Dhagamvar were appointed as members (see Appendix p. 166). The Commission organised a study visit to Vasai block during 9-11 July 1984, visited the many bonded labour-affected villages, and gathered information pertaining to their problems.[4] The report submitted by the Commission supported the cause of the Shramjeevi Sanghatana. The process of identification, release, and rehabilitation of bonded labourers was given to the District Magistrate. A district-level Vigilance Committee was formed under the chairmanship of the District Collector, and Mr. Vivek Pandit was appointed as member by the Supreme Court. Vivek Pandit held this post for a period of 10 years and the Shramjeevi Sanghatana identified and helped release over 1500 bonded labourers and filed almost 465 cases against the "masters" between 1979 and 1993.[5] This was an overwhelming victory for the Shramjeevi Sanghatana.

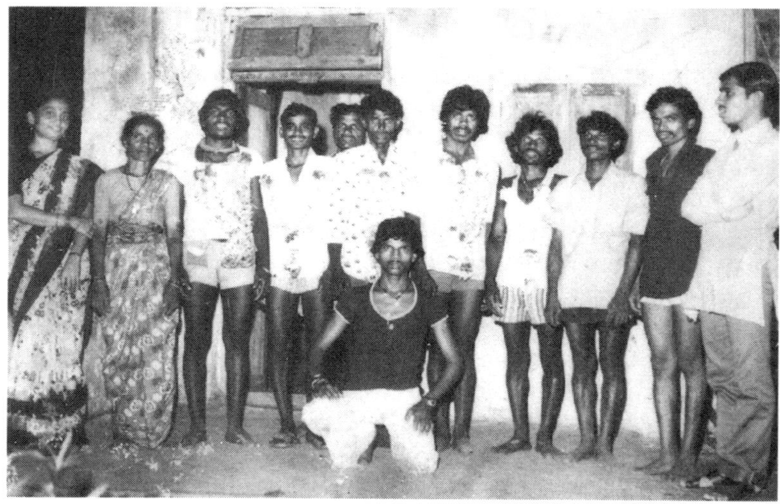

Picture 4.1: *The freed bonded labourers with the leaders of the organisations from Vasai block.*

The organisation helped release *lagingadi* (bonded labourers due to the marriage debt) and fishermen of the Bhatasa river dam. The fishermen *adivasis* were forced to sell their fish to middlemen. They would earn only Rs. 2 to 3 per kg, whereas market rates were Rs. 35 to 40 per kg. The fishermen were not shown their accounts either. This continued for 6 to 7 years. Finally, the activists of the Sanghatana detected bonded labour among the fishermen in Shahapur. The Shramjeevi Sanghatana registered cases against contractors and middlemen with the

Executive Magistrate of Shahapur with the guidance of the District Collector and District Magistrate. The police machinery immediately arrested the contractors and moneylenders and registered the offences. This helped to release 387 fishermen between 1988 and 1990.

Picture 4.2: *During a programme in the year 1984, the proactive support from Justice, Mr. P.N. Bhagwati, Mumbai Commissioner Mr. V. Ranganathan, and the Collector of Thane Mr. Bhaskrao Patil. The picture also shows freed bonded labour Ms. Vimal Pared.*

The initial challenge was to 'release', but, later on the challenge was to 'rehabilitate' the bonded labourers. With the help of the government and the Shramjeevi Sanghatana, the freed bonded labourers registered their own fishing society on December 3, 1993. They registered four fishing societies: *Kothera Zindabad Matsaavyasayik Bahu-uddeshiya Sahakari Society, Dhengalmal Society, Bhatash Society,* and *Kashti Society*. These societies were not limited to one block but covered other blocks as well, namely, Vasai block in Hattipada. A cooperative society of the freed bonded labourers was also set up. It was an important period for the Sanghatana as it had developed its credibility both with the government and among the people. Very soon, people from various villages started approaching the Sanghatana with requests to assist in release of other bonded labourers. Till then, the Sanghatana had helped release more than 5,000 bonded labourers with the help of the government and others.[6]

The Government of Maharashtra helped the Sanghatana in releasing labourers, but the task of rehabilitation remained. This called for inputs for changing mind sets of *adivasis* and preparing them for their own businesses. Traditionally, the government gave freed labourers *Gadi-Jodis* (bullock carts), and the Tahsildar of Vasai taluka had offered them the same but they refused the bullock carts and instead asked for trucks under the Truck Co-operative Society. However, the government was unwilling to accept this request. The Magistrate commented: 'Is there any history of tribals driving trucks? They will want aeroplanes next.' This angered the people who took this up as a challenge. On the occasion of *Makar Sankranti* (a festival of giving and taking sweets made of jaggery), the leader offered them sweets along with a letter of request for the Truck Cooperative Society and requested them to send it to the Prime Minister of India. Permission was granted by the Prime Minister and members registered their Cooperative Truck Society in the village Ambode in Vasai block.

Picture 4.3: *The freed bonded labourers' first truck in Vasai block.*

Imparting training to the societies and its members was a challenge to the Vidhayak Sansad and Shramjeevi Sanghatana, hence they began involving professionals to train the freed labourers to run their societies. *Adivasis* were given training on profit and loss, ways of dealing with customers, and the procedures of record keeping. This helped them in increasing their confidence in running cooperatives. Having the experience of running cooperatives, they experimented with other kinds of societies like brick-kilns, milk cooperative society, agricultural cooperative society, and collective farming for their sustainable livelihood purposes. For helping them build occupational skills for their survival, both the Vidhayak Sansad and the Shramjeevi Sanghatana took up the following programme.

2.1 Training of Members

The organisations developed training methodologies suitable for their members. This section, therefore, describes their training tools and means of understanding human rights and fundamental rights for social justice.

The inhuman treatment given to bonded labourers was the motivation for imparting learning pertaining to dignity and justice. Initially, *adivasis* were not aware about the concept of the struggle for independence but they were aware about their lands being grabbed by the landlords, foresters, and the government under some pretext or the other. They were motivated to reclaim their lands through collective efforts. However, they were timid and had no courage to file cases against their exploitation. The first challenge was to make them able and fearless. Similarly, during the struggle for freedom from bondage, the importance of knowledge and skills was recognised. Therefore, the training had two crucial components: developing perspective and skills. Perspective development involves information, knowledge, mode, and values. Training also focused on social and religious bondage. Developing skills involves training in aspects necessary for the assertion of rights like framing of issues, registering the FIR, preparing the right demands, negotiating with the government and the oppressors, organising and mobilising, strategic planning, media mobilising, leadership development, and taking risks, etc. Orientation on the issues about the judiciary, bureaucracy, legislators, and media were also focused on throughout the training phases. Crucial issues like poverty, indebtedness, fate, superstitions, and ignorance of market realities were discussed during the training. The issues were real issues in their day-to-day lives, which developed their perspective towards the new world.

The training *Shibirs* were four days long. The focus of the training was on developing perspective and skills, which would help in creating fearless human beings, and included issues like police and its duties, revenue officer's duties and rights in releasing bonded labourers, IPC, CRPC, Minimum Wages Act, Prevention of Atrocities Act, and an overview of the Constitution of India. During the first phase, training was given to village, zonal, and block-level activist members.

Adivasis, though willing to work day and night, were reluctant to attend meetings or *Shibirs*. Being unused to sitting down in one place for long, they tended to fall asleep during training. It was an exhausting and a challenging task to make them interested in learning. To combat this, innovative methods of teaching were used during the *Shibirs*. The methods of training included group discussions, individual exercises, role-play, and creating of songs and slogans based on their socio-economic realities. Warli art was used to gain their interest. The facilitators asked members questions and sought answers from them.

In every *Shibir,* members were given the opportunity to share their life experiences. The author happened to be a part of some of the *Shibirs* in village Usgaon and Nirmal. Members shared experiences relating to their bondage and exploitation and recounted incidents like being starved, being fed leftovers, being made to work non-stop by different household members, etc. Some of the activists practised as *Bhagats* before joining these organisations and shared how they fooled people and pretended to use magical powers to cure illnesses. Thus, the trainings taught members how to share experiences and things learned among themselves.

In the *Shibir,* some members wrote songs like *Sharamjeevine jagvala Maharashtra sara aasa zindabad govogavi gajnara* (Shramjeevi Sanghatana has awakened entire Maharashtra and *Zindabad* has spread all over) by Janubhau Meghwale. Another interesting song composed was: *dhawa dhawa dhawa re jameeni lootlaya dhawa re* (hurry up everybody our lands have been grabbed) by Janubhau Meghwale. Songs like these helped to ignite the passion and commitment of activists for the struggle against unjust practices. The Vidhayak Sansad and the Shramjeevi Sanghatana have created several symbols, songs, and slogans as a creative tool of sensitisation among the illiterate communities.

The symbol of the Shramjeevi Sanghatana is *fist*, which is a symbol of unity, solidarity, sense of "we" feeling and integration and collective power. The fist is the symbol of *Zindabad* (victory). The meaning of *Zindabad* is victory of people who can hold their head high always. The symbol of *Zindabad* has become so famous that some members have named their Kirana Store and Cooperative Society as *Zindabad*. Most of the slogans and songs have been created by the leaders and activists of organisations during various agitations. Both Mrs. Venubai Meghwale and Mr. Janubhau Meghwale have penned many of the songs in the Sanghatana. The author observed that all the members greet each other as *Zindabad* instead of Namaskar. This is observed to be the case also in schools, Bal Sanghatana, and *Shibir Shala*, etc.

Picture 4.4: *The Shibir activity of the organisations for their members in Vasai block.*

In many instances, the labourers had never gone outside their villages, or blocks. Their knowledge was limited and they did not have much exposure to other places. The *Shibir* provided an opportunity for them to go out of their hamlets. The

Sahaadhayan Shibir (participatory learning camp) was divided into three categories. The first phase focused on basic orientation. The second pertained to basic learning and opening of new topics. The third phase focused on further details about the topic, reflecting on information to convert it into knowledge, and on the application of this knowledge. Through the last phase, labourers were able to articulate and began thinking of their bondage and its linkage with the ideologies of eminent social thinkers and leaders of the Shramjeevi Sanghatana. The labourers preferred this format to lectures.

Similarly, people became exposed to the main village, with amenities like roads, street lights, drinking water supply, school, flour mills and so on, while in the hamlets where the *adivasis* stayed, no such facilities were available. This helped them to understand the injustice and inequality they faced. They even became equipped to analyse their situation and found that electricity was made available to the powerful people. Whenever outsiders visit villages, they tend to go to the *Patil's* or moneylender's home or the government officer. This made *adivasis* realise the manner in which vested interests operate.

Picture 4.5: *The symbols of the Shramjeevi Sanghatana are fist and Warli art.*

The organisation later changed the venue of the training. They conducted issue-based training directly on farms instead of in closed lecture halls. The issue-based training, included topics like watershed development, land levelling, agricultural activities, crop credit programmes, collective farming, brick-kilns industry, basket making, pigs and goats rearing, running a milk cooperative, and other such activities.

After completing training, members were given field assignments such as a study of their own village or filing a case and getting a copy of the FIR. Use of different methodologies during the action in the field helped members to understand when cooperating was the right action and in which situation resisting was the correct move. They also learned how to use non-violence to overcome opponents. Thus, Mr. Vijay Jadhav, an organiser from the Wada Block carried out an investigation and enquiry of the police's jeep and asked for their vehicle records. It was found that the person driving the jeep was not a police staffer. Activists then filed a case with the police superintendent.

At the office of Shramjeevi Sanghatana a legal-aid meeting was organised weekly. Problems encountered by the *adivasis* were solved through this process. Several people helped Shramjeevi Sanghatana to conduct *Shibirs.* These included the socialist ex-Tahsildar Mr. R.V. Bhuskutebhau, Mr. D.G. Prabhu, Advocate Vijay Sathe and Vidyullata Pandit. Mr. D.G. Prabhu taught members science and the functioning of the human body, etc. Mr. Bhuskutebhau not only trained the members but also wrote many books and booklets in simple language for them. The issue of land regularisation and reclaiming land from non-*adivasis* was an easy task on paper but in practice, it required strengthening through a strategic planning of the Sanghatana. All the trainers mentioned above worked hard, supported the Sanghatana, and were an integral part of the process. Trainers also handed out assignments to the fresh activist members in order to ensure that members get experience and exposure. Assignments included having to visit the police station, the *Talathi* (a village revenue officer), the Gram Sevak, and the Tahsildar (taluka revenue officer).

After training some members filed cases under the Atrocities Act against the "masters" and government officers. They monitored the situation to check whether there was any incidence of violation of the Prevention of Atrocity Act, 1989. They also monitored the implementation of laws like Minimum

Wages, Child Labour, and Bonded Labour, and of fundamental rights and livelihood rights that include land, water, forests and biodiversity. They strongly believe in the slogan 'Educate, organise and agitate' given by Dr. Babasaheb Ambedkar. This was the core of the training programme run by the Vidhayak Sansad and the Shramjeevi Sanghatana.

The author interviewed some of the activists who had completed their participatory learning camps, and observed that these had helped them grow. The *Shibirs* taught them to comprehend a situation in its totality.

An activist member Suresh Renged who lives in village Tilher told the author:

> Earlier we had no confidence to speak to government officers, especially the police and forester and revenue officers, but, later we became equipped to expose the corrupt acts of the Gram Sevak in our village and punish him. We have not only exposed corruption of lower level officers but also that of the taluka officers, especially corruption pertaining to the public distribution system and to the distribution of Below Poverty Line cards. Due to this, officers have changed their communication and style of work.

Here is a case relating to getting a copy of the First Information Report (FIR):

> A woman activist from Bhivandi, Parvati Pawar went to the police station and asked for the copy of FIR for the complaint that she has lodged. The police asked her to revisit the following day. She told him, "you are supposed to give it now and don't ask for a bribe. You have to give me a copy free of cost." The policeman was angry and raised many questions but she did not relent. She answered all questions and said: "Getting a copy of the FIR is our right. Our Constitution has given rights to us as citizens." The police staffer then handed over a copy of the FIR to her.

The first freed bonded labourers had become the leaders of the Vidhayak Sansad and the Shramjeevi Sanghatana and directed participation in local self-governance. Mr. Lahu Pasari shared his experience:

> When I participated in the *Shibir* at Tilsa village, I realised the process of exploitation, and became aware about the inequality in hamlets and villages. I obtained information about different

> laws and this enabled me to handle cases of other poor *adivasis*. Most important was the knowledge I got about the rest of the world. This helped reduce my fear and increased my confidence to hold my head high when dealing with *Patils* and *Pudharis* (traditional power centres of the villages) in the society. I travelled to Delhi by flight for the meetings of the Labour Commission and the *Bandhua Mukti Morcha* (Movement of bonded labour release by Swami Agnivesh). I was very glad when I boarded the aircraft for the Delhi trip. It was my first flying experience and was memorable in my life. At the Delhi airport a policeman started harassing me when I went to the toilet. Vivekbhau immediately intervened and showed the details of my tickets. Vivekbhau argued with the policeman and resolved the matter. That experience gave me courage to talk with the policemen and I decided to work with them. After that incident, I have decided to solve the problems of other *adivasis* regarding the police and run a legal-aid centre for them. I think the *Patils* and the "masters", have realised that we are also human beings and that is our victory.

Thus, one can surmise that the process of *Shibirs* developed Shramjeevi Sanghatana's cadres for the development of their society. The *Shibir* is a continuous activity of the Sanghatana and is meant for the newcomers of the Sanghatana as well. The prominent members from amongst the first batch of the cadres have become president and chairman of the Vidhayak Sansad and the Shramjeevi Sanghatana. Many of the members have positions of secretary, general secretary, and head of the department of the various sections in different programmes. Mr. Janubhau Meghwale, Mr. Lahu Pasari, Mr. R.V. Bhuskute, Mrs. Venubai Meghwale, Mr. Keshav Nankar and others had become the presidents of the Shramjeevi Sanghatana.

Another aspect of the training pertained to creating and developing assets such as land and agriculture. Separate programmes were launched for these. These include the following.

A. The Training for the Watershed Development Programme

Shramjeevi Sanghatana realised that there was a need for agricultural and watershed training to enable members to develop their own land. The immediate need of members was for adequate food. Initially, Vidhayak Sansad and Shramjeevi Sanghatana initiated the *Khavati* (foodgrains) programme to distribute ration to the members. As a part of rehabilitation of *adivasis,* they developed a separate section in the village Usgaon. The village watershed programme was initiated in Vasai block. Mr. Mahesh Hindlekar and Mr. Ramesh Chouthe undertook the watershed development work in the eastern belt of Vasai block. These programmes were replicated in the villages, viz. Medhe, Karjon, Aadne, Kelipada, Tilher, and Usgaon.

The watershed development programme was initiated in 1991 to rehabilitate freed bonded labourers. The main aim of the programme was to help the marginal and small farmers, fisherfolk, farm labourers, and landless people in getting employment. The objectives of the programme were to improve the economic condition of the *adivasis*, in general, and the bonded labourers, in particular. The conservation of soil, water, and forests was required both to generate wages at the village level and to bring land under cultivation. The initial challenge was to make lands cultivable, because the lands were infertile, rocky, and uneven. Land levelling and *nullah* bunding works were done to begin with. Later, small dams, percolation tanks, contour building, and digging of wells was taken up.

The watershed development trainings were organised in different hamlets on a rotation basis so that all members could get a chance to organise and participate. The resultant land treatment measures resulted in an increase in the area brought under cultivation by the members. A large number of members benefited and this was quite evident in the village Tilher where most of the members were no longer worried about their food security. They cultivated high yielding varieties on their farms. Their agricultural output has increased from 2 to 20 quintals. Now, they did not need to borrow or take government's *Khavati* for their subsistence. The watershed development programme helped not only to raise the productivity of their lands but also to generate employment within the village, especially during the lean season.

B. The Training for the Agriculture Development Programme

The agriculture development programme was launched in 1983-

1984 in Vasai block for the rehabilitation of freed bonded labourers who desired to develop lands and cultivate them well. Keeping this in mind, the Vidhayak Sansad developed a grain bank that maintained fertilisers, seeds and plants supplies for farmers. Also the Vidhayak Sansad adopted the method of collective farming. The first freed bonded labour, Mr. Keshav Nankar took up the challenge to handle the agriculture development programme in the Vasai block. Mr. Nankar initiated collective farming in various villages to grow watermelons, vegetables, groundnuts, green fodder, bananas, sapota, and fisheries.

Initially, members received training from outsiders, especially from the agriculture specialists. Then they continued their training and research under the guidance of Keshavbhau Nankar. The members of the Shramjeevi Sanghatana, Mr. Rambhau Warana, Mr. Kondu Sambare, and Mr. Laxman Kom paid maximum attention to the agricultural activities in Kajupada and elsewhere. The idea of cooperative farming emerged from Mr. Keshav Nankar, who had experience of cultivating watermelons and vegetables. This experiment empowered them to earn more than Rs. one lakh a year.

Picture 4.6: *The watershed bandhara (a tank) activity in Vasai block.*

Earlier, the members were not able to identify the appropriate seeds. Sometimes, they were cheated by the traders and they had to pay more money for getting seeds and pesticides. The unit of the agriculture of Vidhayak Sansad helped in training and capacity building of the members. The impact of the training and experiment in villages was quite evident in Kajupada, Kelipada, Varthapada, and Medhe, where they developed various varieties of floriculture and as many as 114 types of medicinal plants..

The agricultural programme enabled many ex-bonded labourers to invest their labour in land leased or borrowed for the seasonal cultivation of vegetables, grains, and watermelons. The agricultural department of the organisation was working towards provision of lift irrigation facilities to enable cultivation of a second crop during the dry season and had even developed fishing ponds in Kajupada. The special interest of *adivasis* in fishing led to developing this novel type of fishing.

Picture 4.7: *The agriculture activity undertaken by the organisations in Vasai block.*

In the last 25 years, the Vidhayak Sansad and the Shramjeevi Sanghatana implemented various activities for agricultural development, which resulted in enhancing the economic and social condition of the members. The positive impact of the agricultural programme on members was clear as growth of their agricultural assets as well as housing assets was observed. Changes in their economic life helped in improving their quality of life and making them optimistic.

In addition to the above-mentioned trainings, the members were given training in poultry production and pigs and goats rearing. Besides, they were given training for leadership development. The following section is devoted to the aspect of the leadership development training programme.

2.2 Leadership Development of the Members

As seen, training for human development was an important factor and played a crucial role in the lives of *adivasis*. Leadership is the most important aspect of any organisation or institution. The leadership development programme for the organisations was a product of evolution as the organisations dealt with changing situations. Activist leaders emerged through processes that include Bal Sanghatana, camps, *morcha*, *dharna*, and issue-based training programmes. The current lot of leaders and activists said that they were inspired by Sane Guruji, S.M. Joshi, Martin Luther King Jr, Mahatma Gandhi, Dr. Babasaheb Ambedkar, and Rosa Parks.

The founding leaders of the Shramjeevi Sanghatana used methods and tactics of Paulo Freire (*Pedagogy of the Oppressed*), Sun Tsu (*The Art of War*), and Saul Alinsky (*Rules for Radicals and Reviles for Radicals*) in developing innovative strategies in each struggle. Leadership that creates space for others to develop and leads towards the appropriate goals is important in people's organisations.

The cadre of the Shramjeevi Sanghatana grew and later became leaders and activists. These leaders identified people's issues and concerns and had the ability to empathise and perceive the members' problems as their own. They were interactive and discussed methods with their followers and took the necessary action to tackle the problems. They therefore earned the trust and respect of the members who felt close to these leaders and activists. The members accepted them as leaders because of qualities like perspective and skills in organising people and negotiating with government officers. Leaders displayed a readiness to act and empathised with members over incidents of injustice and exploitation. Leaders showed qualities like a risk taking capacity, a positive attitude, willingness to sacrifice, and the ability to identify the opponent's weakness. The leaders of the Vidhayak Sansad and Shramjeevi Sanghatana devoted their lives to the development of poor *adivasis*. The membership of the Sanghatana increased to over 22,000 in the year 2007.

Members who have observed the work of leaders and activists have seen them walk the talk. Action is the essence of grassroots leadership and members are capable of evaluating the qualities of leaders such as articulation skills, risk taking, taking ownership of the problem, etc. Mr. Vivek Pandit listed some of the essential qualities that a leader must have. He said that an effectives grassroots leader must be a patient listener, be able to make friends easily, have the capacity to be articulate, be self-disciplined, be able to set limits, have vision, and have a good sense of humour.[7] In the Shramjeevi Sanghatana, those capable of taking action and possessing negotiation skills while dealing with decision-makers and opponents are considered as potential leaders. The ability to take action and take risks enhances leadership potential. Additionally, leaders and activists conduct participatory discussions on issues faced by members to formulate questions and demands around an issue. For example, the fact that bonded labourers do not want their children to suffer their fate. is an attitudinal change that has occurred through inputs given by the leaders and activists who have made members think about their bondage and slavery.

For guaging the requirements of the participants, activists conducted training programmes in the local language along with visual aids. Most of the members were illiterate. Hence mechanisms like plays based on their life stories, simulations, group discussions, field exposure, games and other participatory methods were used in trainings. Assignments were given to enable members to learn through practice. Activities included issue based letter or memorandum writing to the concerned government machinery, and carrying out dialogue with government officers.

One such effective leader and activist, named Mr. Balaram Bhoir, who, at the time of the survey, was the General Secretary of the Shramjeevi Sanghatana had studied only up to grade seven but displayed qualities like courage when dealing with government officials as well as the judiciary and was able to expose corruption in the Special Executive Magistrate office in the Bhivandi block. For instance, a Katkari tribal was tortured and was asked to pay money to a clerk in the Court. Mr. Balaram heard about this. He approached the concerned clerk and demanded an apology and followed it up by going to the police station to register an atrocity case against the clerk. The police phoned the Special Executive Magistrate and enquired about the matter but the clerk in question apologised to the person who had been wronged before the matter went further. Mr. Bhoir had cordial relations with the Scheduled Caste and Scheduled Tribe departments in the districts of Thane, Nashik, and Raigad. The author once observed the process of negotiations by Mr. Bhoir with the Tribal Development Commissioner on the issue of adequate budget for the educational programme of drop-out children.

Shramjeevi Sanghatana and Vidhayak Sansad organise training programmes for the activists to update their knowledge on changing laws, schemes, and accordingly, activists are able to work out appropriate strategies. Apart from training adult activists, the Bal Sanghatana is an important activity for youth development and leadership within the community. The activity was started in 1995 in the five talukas, viz. Vasai, Wada, Bhivandi, Shahapur, and Vikramgarh. Similarly, many activities for children are carried out in the Ashram School, Zilla Parishad School, Bhonga Shala, and Mukt Shala. The activities include special sports training, a Bal Krida Melawa or sports competition for children, and essay writing. The idea of youth training has the objective of creating a cadre of decent human beings. The study classes aim at imparting knowledge on subjects such as laws, rights, which will aid the youth to become self-reliant and equipped to fight against injustice (see Appendix p. 174).

The Vidhayak Sansad opened student branches in the entire village where the Shramjeevi Sanghatana members were present. Hundreds of youth have become members of the Bal Sanghatana. During the year of 2006-07 more than 1,425 students participated in various activities and benefited from the 74 branches of this Sanghatana in Thane district.[8] Classes are held at night. Students receive orientation in social justice, human rights, and the Constitution. The Vidhayak Sansad organises trainings and gives exposure to the youth, especially for the Bal Sanghatana members.

Picture 4.8: *The students of Bal Sanghatana in Vasai block.*

More than 1,500 students benefited from the various programmes such as provision of educational equipment, study tours, mobile library, science exhibition, Warli art camps, celebration of national festivals, plantation for social forestry, and recreation and sports assembly. These youth can later become members of the Shramjeevi Sanghatana and become leaders and activists. The current lot of the taluka organisers and secretaries are composed mostly of those that studied in the Bal Sanghatana.

The Vidhayak Sansad initiated youth leadership programmes with a view to ensure that children grow up to be empowered and do not suffer exploitation. The Bal Sanghatana also identified and exposed cases of superstitions in the Shahapur block in 1995. Thus, auction of women was stopped by the youth. They were also able to prevent child marriage cases in several villages. Similarly the bad conditions of schools were exposed and, monitoring the quality of the Mid-day Meal was carried out. Additionally, the inadequate resources in health camps were identified. Youth leaders use the instrument of non-violence and *satyagraha*. The corruption in the Mid-day Meal Schemes in Vasai, Wada, and Shahapur blocks was eliminated.

For this, members met the education development officers, and submitted a memorandum. Overall, the youth leadership is being built as a result of the various training programmes and activities run both by the Vidhayak Sansad and the Shramjeevi Sanghatana. The Minister of Social Justice at the time, Mr. Chandrakant Handore had visited the programmes and was impressed by the *adivasi* children.

As seen, the leadership development is a crucial part of conscientisation. Through the dialogue and orientation, the youth who were illiterate have now become self-reliant and empowered. Another important aspect is organising and mobilising people, and people's participation in action, which helps them to assert their rights.

The next part will focus on members' organising and mobilising for participation in various actions such as *dharna* (sit-ins or continuous demonstration), *morcha* (protest rally), *satyagraha, rasta roko* (jamming the roads), fasting, rallies, and *melawas* (conventions).

3. People's Organising, Mobilising and Participation in Action

As noted, since the last 25 years, the Shramjeevi Sanghatana and Vidhayak Sansad have been organising the unorganised ex-untouchables, *adivasis,* and other backward communities in the study area for social justice, human rights and development. Organising and mobilising have been their strength. The process of organising and mobilising has played a key role in conscientisation of the oppressed communities. This section focuses on tactics and strategies for the organising and mobilising for social causes.

After helping to release bonded labourers, the task of organising these labourers and mobilising them on issues/ events/activities have been ongoing. Since the Shramjeevi Sanghatana started with helping to release bonded labourers, the mobilisation of people at that time was based on their identity as bonded labourers. The commonality of people's interests, identity, issues, and problems helped the organisation in organising and mobilising these people. In recent times, the focus has been shifting from identity as bonded labourers that of landless labourers, farm workers, EGS workers, or unorganised labourers in general. Thus, the scope has now widened.

Picture 4.9: *The members of the Shramjeevi Sanghatana have participated in a protest for the land rights.*

The rights-based approach was used in organising and mobilising to enable people to understand the fundamental rights, duties and directive principles of the state enshrined in the Constitution. The focus of the organisations was on understanding the Constitution, approaching the legislators for introduction of relevant laws, engaging the existing executive system for the implementation of laws and welfare programmes, approaching the judiciary, and creating social action groups to put pressure on existing machinery. Thus, through their orientation process, they make people aware about their rights and powers. Their focus is to solve problems through people's power. This builds a sense of social service in the members. Successful campaigns motivate local persons to try to solve problems of others. Success is reflected through the reclaiming of their land rights from the landlords. People have learnt to formulate their issues and oppose power structures and confront them. They have learnt to become united.

Organising people involves bringing about a sense of solidarity, integrity, equality, brotherhood, and a sense of belonging. Organising people from different castes, religions, and other background helps eliminate barriers. In Shramjeevi Sanghatana, there are no barriers of caste, ethnicity, religion, etc.

Their grassroots organising is based on the Constitutional principles but often puts them against the system which is why the emphasis on non-violence is imperative. Discipline was ensured such that organised members do not resort to violence but sort out issues through democratic means. Ensuring that members do not get provoked and do not react physically or even use abusive language, abuse women in general, etc, was an important aspect of organising people. This was done through imparting values and norms and in-depth discussion and debate with the members.

Delegation or representation has been their strength as has been their ability to get the attention of the government machinery which leads to further discussion. Delegated representatives that meet the concerned authorities ensure that they keep members informed and updated. The process is useful for negotiating on the issues of rehabilitation of bonded labourers, demands for minimum wages, and land regularisation. It is also useful in identifying the appropriate negotiator and influencing concerned policy makers and implementers. This process was used in all the campaigns, as a strategy for demanding and fulfilling people's aspirations. It was also useful in mobilising people's opinions and for sharpening ideas to focus on the issues. The Sanghatana has made several representations to the Members of Parliament (MP), the Members of the Legislative Assembly (MLA), Ministers of various departments, bureaucrats, including executives, judiciary authorities, for seeking rights and justice.

Morchas

Organising and mobilising people for a *morcha* or protest rally was one of the strengths of the Shramjeevi Sanghatana. The *morcha* enables exerting pressure on concerned government officers' and people's representatives and is an instrument for displaying the strength of people as well as a mechanism that makes concerned authorities talk about the issues and attempt to solve them. For organising and mobilising people for the *morcha,* the Shramjeevi Sanghatana would identify the affected, friends, and well-wishers, who would be able to support their cause, and participate.

On July 12, 2005 a huge *morcha* was organised in front of the District Collector's office Thane, with more than 20,000 members.[9] The *morcha* was organised by Shramjeevi Sanghatana for the rights of *adivasis* to lands belonging to them, which they had been cultivating for several generations.

For the preparation of the *morcha,* members and activists mobilised people who were affected and sympathisers/well-wishers to support the issue. Logistics like required instruments such as placards, banners, microphones, battery, pamphlets, and memorandum were taken care of at the planning stage. Similarly, planning also involved ensuring maximum women's participation and establishing the correct dress code. After the planning stage, they took permission from the police officer and Executive Magistrate. This included taking permission for the rally at least 24 hours before the event and permission for the use of the microphone. They additionally organised press meetings before the action. They made lists of participants for their convenience and observed discipline to avoid any kind of untoward incident.

During the *morcha* or rally, volunteers took care of participants' requirements like water, food, and medicines. When they received a call from the negotiator they maintained transparency and openness and informed protesters. Often when only leaders were invited for talks and negotiations, they insisted that a larger group would represent their side during talks. This enhanced the spirit of collectivity among the protestors. When a break-off group left the protest to meet and negotiate with policy makers, other activists from the group ensured that motivation of those waiting did not wane. This was done through ongoing speeches, songs, and slogans. The author observed that immense planning and organisation went into any event of this kind.

Picture 4.10: *The strength of Shramjeevi Sanghatana members who participated in the morcha.*

Gheraos

The Sanghatan also used the *gherao* method on many occasions. *Gherao* actions are aimed at forcing and influencing authorities to take immediate favourable decisions. The author observed the Ganeshpuri Melawa on the occasion of Independence Day in the year 2003. The Tahsildar of Bhivandi refused to act against illegal encroachment/construction on the public road built by Gurudev Siddhapeeth. A *gherao* was hence done for bringing about immediate action. Activists approached the Block Development Officer and the Sub-Divisional Officer along with their huge following with their demands. During a *gherao,* members or activists must be mobilised at short notice and hence this approach is used occasionally since it involves an element of risk as there is no time for planning and organising in advance. Additionally, arrests can take place during a *gherao* but activists have always been prepared for that.

Dharnas

Another mechanism used is the *dharna* (sit-ins) with the available number of people and this is used when authorities are not responsive to people's demands. The *dharna* can sometimes become an indefinite one. During a *dharna,* activists use banners, posters, and pamphlets to highlight the issue and attract media attention. Usually, it is organised at block, district, and state levels.

Picture 4.11: *The members of the Shramjeevi Sanghatana sitting in dharna for their demands in Vasai block.*

The author observed a few of these *dharna*s which were done for issues such as getting ration cards, regularisation of lands, receiving necessary civic amenities, and getting justice in case of atrocities on *adivasis* and women. *Dharnas* require extensive pre-planning. This includes arrangement of the sitting area in the shade and other such matters. To retain the spirit of protestors, speeches of members and invitees from outside the organisation are often arranged. Many activists have composed songs and slogans during the *dharna* programmes.

Rasta Roko Agitations

Another important instrument used is *rasta roko* (Jamming the roads). To influence decision-makers, *rasta roko,* was used by the Sanghatana. This mechanism requires a large number of people. Using this mechanism, activists were able to tackle many issues. These included getting caste certificates, getting educational equipment, and permission for appearing for school examinations. Sometimes, *rasta roko* was done for several hours till demands were fulfilled by the concerned departments.

Rasta roko was done on the Mumbai-Ahmedabad highway when the issue concerned levying of the illegal toll charge for road maintenance. Now, the practice of levying the toll charges has been stopped and the road maintenance is done from time to time.

Similarly, using *rasta roko,* activists were able to get the authorities to cancel the privatisations of the state transport (ST) services in the Vasai block, which had issued a tender to give the service contract to private companies. For accomplishing cancellation of privatisation of ST services, activists first carried out a time-bound fast but that did not work, after which they carried out *rasta roko* with more than 5,000 members of the Shramjeevi Sanghatana. *Rasta roko* was done on the Mumbai-Ahmedabad highway for five days during December 11-15, 2005. When even this did not yield the appropriate response from the government, several activists went on an indefinite fast after which the issuing of tenders was cancelled by the authorities.

Satyagrahas

When other instruments fail to work, activists use *satyagraha* as passive resistance. Mahatma Gandhi used this tool and won the battle against the British Government. *Satyagraha* is used when there are very serious issues and there is a need to make the concerned authorities ethically aware. During *satyagraha,* power is equally shared among the protesters and individual members are given equal importance. This gives members a feeling of collectiveness and a sense of contribution to the cause. During *satyagrahas.* the police can use physical force but activists must not react with violence in these circumstances.

Satyagrahas were organised for issues that included: effective implementation of various policies and laws, GR (Government Resolution) and amendments to a policy or rules in addition to monitoring of civic amenities and individual benefits to the members. The first *satyagraha* was organised in village Depivali on August 15, 1983 to get the feel of independence and freedom.

The government had penalised the *adivasis* for singing the *Rashtrageet* (national anthem) and saluting the *Tiranga* (National Flag hoisting) without prior permission. At that time, the freed bonded labourers were not aware about freedom and independence, but, with the help of the Shramjeevi Sanghatana they were made aware about the value of freedom.

On August 15, 1984, they were stopped from flag hoisting in front of the school by the ex-MLA Mr. Thakur. However, with the organised strength of the members, they went ahead with flag hoisting. During this event, many members were brutally beaten by the police. Many activists were sent to jail for eight days but did so with the slogans and songs of Mahatma Gandhi, Bhagat Singh, Dr. Ambedkar, and Sane Guruji . The first cadre and leaders went to jail and refused bail as they had not committed any offence. With efforts from the Hon. MLA Mr. Sadanand Varde and reporters of print media, activists agreed to post bail. It was the first successful *satyagraha* in the lives of *adivasis*.

Since then, every year, more than 15,000 members celebrate flag hoisting in village Vajreshawari which is known for the successful *satyagraha* for the rights of minimum wages to *adivasis*. There was an uprising against Gurudev Siddhapeeth in Ganeshpuri village on April 19, 1987 for the rights to minimum wages and equal wages to men and women. The Shramjeevi Sanghatana carried out a 33-day *satyagraha* for the rights of minimum wages. It is thus clear that without mass mobilisation it would not have been possible to resist the existing illegal practices.

A significant victory regarding minimum wages was achieved in Vedhe village. At that time the minimum wage was only Rs. 7 but people were not given even Rs. 4 or Rs. 5. In Aadne village, they were given only Rs. 2. The labourers unanimously decided that unless and until they were given minimum wages, they would not work on anybody's farm. During that period, many *satyagrahas* were done in front of houses of the landowners. This helped them get the right compensation. In Vedhe village, almost 150 activists were sent to jail and these included women with their children.

Picture 4.12: *The activists of the Shramjeevi Sanghatana during the satyagraha in Mumbai.*

Similarly, the Shramjeevi Sanghatana carried out many *satyagrahas* for helping *adivasi*s to obtain caste/tribe-related certificates. Owing to lack of awareness, the Katkaris were often cheated by the landlords and were not given certificates necessary for availing of the benefits of government schemes. With the help of the Shramjeevi Sanghatana, many *adivasis* got their tribe certificates. At that time, more than 5,000 *adivasis* participated in the *satyagraha*. Government officials asked *adivasis* for their birth and school-leaving certificates to which *adivasis* raised the question "has there been any school for *adivasis?*" Eventually *adivasis* were able to show the proof of them being *adivasis* using their cultural instruments to the district collector. Eventually, the government had to consider their traditional culture and their lifestyle and issued certificates of scheduled tribes to *adivasis*. It was observed that in the study village, all the members got their certificates. All the members also got their ration cards as their proof of residence. That is why they have access to the schemes meant for them and have become eligible for getting benefits of schemes relating to education, health, agriculture equipment, maternity and so on. Because of success, using various agitation mechanisms, people approached the Shramjeevi Sanghatana to become members. Thus it gained many supporters, friends, volunteers, and new activists. This built confidence and led to the building of leadership as well.

4. The Role of People-centred Advocacy and Lobbying

Apart from these strategies for organising, mobilising, and action, other mechanisms like advocacy and lobbying and bridging the gap between grassroots and state for policy making were also used. It is therefore necessary to discuss the status of advocacy and lobbying for the larger impact on the lives of *adivasis*.

The process of advocacy was pioneered in India in the 1990s. A team of young enthusiastic people's organisations' activists received training from the Advocacy Institute, Washington, and reflected their experience in their work in advocacy and organising and mobilising. The process of advocacy involves collective action to achieve the collective goal. In the advocacy process, activists focus on democratic spaces through legislative advocacy, judiciary, working with executives, and media.

The author observed advocacy as a process of enhancing people's lives and empowering them through the assertions of their rights. The expertise of the Sanghatana in organising and mobilising using non-violent mechanisms helped in influencing the decision-makers and government to evolve policies and government resolutions in the interest of bonded labourers, i.e. releasing and rehabilitating, giving employment under the employment guarantee scheme, education for all, and rights to forest lands.

Both the Sanghatana and the Sansad used planned and organised strategies. Later, they started advocacy capacity building for their activists. They realised that while the Advocacy Institute taught them theory, they were using advocacy in their day-to-day activities. They arrived at a balance between theory and practice in their work.

In addition, other people's organisation and advocacy organisations were initiated and strengthened by the Vidhayak Sansad and the Shramjeevi Sanghatana. These include the *Manavi Hakka Abhiyan* (Campaign for Human Rights, Beed),

Samarthan (Advocacy, Mumbai) and National Centre for Advocacy Studies, Pune. Besides, there are other organisations and individuals, which gathered support for their cause and struggle for the rights of *adivasis*.

Lobbying is a process to brief people's representatives during the session in the lobby of legislative premises. This important tool is also used while advocating the rights of the poor. The leaders of these organisations have trained all their young activists. They focus on the government systems such as the legislature, executive, judiciary, and also on the media. In legislature, they focus on state, parliament, and their organisations and functions, local self-governance in the Panchayati Raj, the role of elected representatives, the role of bureaucracy and their dynamics. In the executive system, the topics of discussion are roles, responsibilities, and process of recruitment, structure of executives and how they can be persuaded. In the judiciary, the subject is structure and functions of the judiciary, the level of courts, their powers, and quasi-judiciary bodies such as the National Human Rights Commission, State Human Rights Commission, the Women's Commission, Minority Commission and their powers and duties.

Special emphasis is laid on media, which creates people's opinions and helps obtain the support of the larger public for various causes. In media, they focus on the types of media, use of media, newspapers' policy, the nature of different columns of the press, organising press meets and conferences, press releases, and so on.

Additionally, they deliberate upon the police system and its structure and duties, Police Act, accountability, criminal justice system, and access to the police. As there are matters pertaining to the revenue department, they discuss the revenue system, the Land Revenue Code, Land Rights Act, Land Reform, land holding pattern, struggles over land rights, land disputes and rights, poor people's problems related to lands and the protection of common people's land. Such are the topics, which are taught in the capacity-building process of advocacy.

Advocacy training was not only organised for the activists of the Shramjeevi Sanghatana but also for the activists of other organisations all over the state and at the national level. Since the organisations not only developed capacities of the activists but also shouldered various campaigns for their rights, the following section is devoted to the nature of the campaign as the focal point of organisations.

A. The Campaign for the Release of Bonded Labourers

As noted, the Vidhayak Sansad and the Shramjeevi Sanghatana have used the rights-based approach for people-centred advocacy and for organising people for the right to freedom from bondage, freedom from atrocity, freedom from tyrannical landlords, and moneylenders, and to become fearless human beings. To abolish the bonded labour system, the government had enacted the Bonded Labour (Abolition) Act, 1976, but despite this, the bonded labour system was prevalent in Thane district until 1984.

As we have noted, the Government of Maharashtra was unwilling to accept the continuing practice of bonded labour in the state. Therefore, the Shramjeevi Sanghatana identified more than 1500 Lagingadi and Machhimar *Vethbeegar* (debt of marriage and fisherfolk bonded labourers) in Vasai, Wada, Shahapur, and Bhiwandi blocks of Thane district. The bonded labourers belonged to ages ranging from 10 to 64 years. The bonded labourers were bonded for periods ranging from 1 month to 50 years. In some cases, entire families were bonded labourers.

Through the process of organising labourers and spreading awareness about their slavery activists were able to mobilise support from well-wishers and sensitive people from the judiciary, executive, media, academicians, artists and others to support their cause. It was not an easy task to challenge moneylenders, but the leaders and activists persisted.

Morchas, *dharnas*, and *satyagrahas* were carried out as noted previously and activists also approached the High Court and Supreme Court in order to ensure release and rehabilitation of bonded labourers. It has been noted previously that the organisations helped release 1,500 bonded labourers in 1984 in Vasai block.[10] Details of how this was accomplished are as follows.

The Ministry of Labour held consultations with the Shramjeevi Sanghatana for the release of bonded labourers in the state. The government was unwilling to act against the culprits, but the Labour Minister, Mr. Ajit Nimbalkar issued a letter to the District Collector to incorporate the names of Mr. Vivek and Mrs. Vidyutllata Pandit in the Bonded Labour Vigilance Committee. Mr. Nimbalkar also visited Thane to enquire about the status of the Committee. As a member of the Committee, Mr. Vivek Pandit wrote a hundred-page report and sent it to the Supreme Court Justice, Mr. P.N. Bhagwati. Immediately, Justice Bhagwati appointed a Commission of Dr. Vasudha Dhagamwar and Dr. Satyaranjan Sathe for a detailed enquiry. The impact of the Commission's report helped in the release of bonded labourers in the district. Given guidelines from the Supreme Court and Commission, the district collector, revenue department and the police department helped the Shramjeevi Sanghatana. Thus, judiciary and executive advocacy resulted in the release of bonded labourers. The then Tahsildar, Mr. R.V. Bhuskutebhau also assisted in this endeavour. Many legislators also paid adequate attention towards the cause and supported the issue, raising questions in the state assembly. Often, socialist Mr. G. P. Pradhan and Prof. Sadanand Varde discussed issues with Members of the both the Legislative Assembly and Council. Thus, the role of legislative advocacy played an important role in solving the larger problem (see Appendix p. 173).

Picture 4.13: *The adivasi family released by the Shramjeevi Sanghatana in Vasai block.*

The importance of media cannot be ignored in struggles of this nature. The print media played a crucial role in highlighting the issues in their newspapers, which included the *Maharashtra Times, Sakal, Loksatta, The Indian Express,* and *The Times of India.* Using this multi-pronged approach, the Shramjeevi Sanghatana helped to release 23 bonded labourers' families in the Vasai block. [11] It was the process of collective advocacy for the rights of *adivasis.* Many activists and members from the study village participated in the special campaign against the bonded labour system, and obtained their own release as well as that of others.

The freed bonded labourers sang a song of freedom: *Pandhara August dis ujadla Depivali gavala, 84 salala ghadun gela ek itihas, polisanchi modli khod hamkhas, patlani rokhun dharle shawasas ji..ji.* (The day of 15th August in village Depivali has risen in the year 1984 and has created the history of freedom of bonded labourers. They had shown their strength against the police, *Patils* and local powerful persons.)

They experience true freedom when they hoisted the Indian flag for the first time in the village Depivali on August 15, 1984. It was by hoisting the flag that the organisations celebrated the release of bonded labourers. For helping release landed labourers, the leaders of organisations were conferred with the Anti-Slavery Award in London in 1999.

Picture 4.14: *The leaders of the Shramjeevi Sanghatana during the award ceremony in London in 1999.*

B. The Campaign for the Right to Education

The author observed an important development programme of education of children in the study area. The methodology of the programme was not just service delivery but to create political consciousness among the *adivasi* children. To get their educational rights they employed various methods to build up pressure on the state government.

An interesting struggle carried out was that for the right to education so as to eradicate child labour and involve the government in imparting education to the drop-out and out-of-school children. In order to provide education for the brick-kiln workers' children the Sanghatana initiated innovative educational programmes in the study area and over Thane district. Once they started to fulfil the need of their livelihood they took up the challenge of giving education to the children in the district. Traditionally, since schools were not available in hamlets, children were engaged in tending to cattle and looking after their siblings. It was therefore difficult to begin the educational programme where the history of education was lacking and there was no awareness about education.

Keeping in mind the larger goal to improve the education among the *adivasis* the Sanghatana and Sansad initiated innovative programmes and this then was reflected in the policy and supported by the government. When the government authorities agreed to take responsibility of drop-out and out-of-school children the Vidhayak Sansad and the Shramjeevi Sanghatana began a schooling programme in the Vasai block. The Vidhayak Sansad began the education programme in 1995-96 through the *Bhonga Shala, Mukt Shala, Vasti Shala, Shibir Shala,* and Study Classes in hamlets with the aim of reducing child labour, preventing migration, preventing dropping out of schools, imparting value education, which would lead them towards becoming good human beings and responsible citizens of the nation. To make the government accountable, the Sansad pressurised the government machinery to implement the right to education.

Picture 4.15: *The Bhonga Shala activity in Vasai block.*

With the efforts of the Vidhayak Sansad, a survey was conducted to find out the status of the children between 6 and 14 years of Thane district in the year 2000. The survey was conducted in three blocks including Wada, Bhiwandi, and Shahapur, in 300 hamlets. The survey found that more than 3,000 children who were out of school, were engaged in brick-kilns and were looking after their siblings. With these data along with video documentation, they could put pressure on the government for the policy of *Mukt Shala* and *Vasti Shala* all over the district and state. The state government had not made any provision for the drop-out children in the state budget and did not fulfil the promises given to the Vidhayak Sansad. To make the then Shiv Sena and BJP government accountable, a huge *morcha* was organised on March 12, 1999.[12] More than 2,000 activists and child labourers staged a protest on the Azad Maidan and solicited people for donations for their education. Using huge baskets, children asked for donations in the areas of the fort and Mantralaya of Mumbai and collected a sum of Rs. 1,030. While requesting donations, they used the slogan *sarkarla lagliya bhik an mulana mhantaya shik* (government is penniless and yet ask children to go to the school).

At that time, Mr. Manohar Joshi was the Chief Minister of Maharashtra. He immediately appointed a task force of three members including Mr. Vivek Pandit (of Vidhayak Sansad, Shramjeevi Sanghatana, and Samarthan), Mr. Dilip Gogte (Asst. Director of Primary Education), and Ms. Vijaya Chauhan of (UNICEF).[13]

According to the National Education Scheme 1998, and the State Plan of Action, 1994 for the universalisation of education, the *Mukta Shala* and Mahatma Phule Shikshan Hami Yojana are deemed the best option(s) where other education schemes are not available. The *Mukta Shala* scheme was suggested to the state government both by the Vidhayak Sansad and the Shramjeevi Sanghatana based on the above. However, despite follow up with the government, the *Mukta Shala* scheme and Mahatma Phule Shikshan Hami Yojana were not implemented.

Again, activists organised a *Kori Pati Morcha* (blank slate agitation) at August Kranti Maidan, Mumbai, on August 14, 2000.

Picture 4.16: *The drop-out children in agitation for their right to education in Mumbai.*

At this rally, more than 5,000 underprivileged children held flags and shouted slogans: *swatantrachi lavli pati, aamchi thevali kori pati* (a banner of independence has been put up, but our slate has been kept blank). During the *Kori Pati Morcha* the children brought their goats with them. On the same day, 14th August, the Chief Minister Mr. Vilasrao Deshmukh assured the Vidhayak Sansad and the Shramjeevi Sanghatana that they were permitted to open schools from October 2, 2000. It was an assurance not only made to the children in Thane district but also to all the 66 lakh children aged between 6 and 14 years in the state who were unable to get access to schools.[14] The government then enacted the *Mukta Shala* and Mahatma Phule Shikshan Hami Yojana all over the state from October 2, 2000.

For this campaign for the right to education, the organisations obtained support from the legislators, executives, and overwhelming support from the media who kept up the pressure and carried out a watchdog role on the government's actions. The media campaign sensitised many reporters and got coverage with the support of Samarthan Mumbai. The strategy of protesting at the right time helped in getting the government to act. It was the strength of the Vidhayak Sansad, Shramjeevi Sanghatana, and Samarthan that pressurised the government into creating a holistic policy at the state level. Thus, people-centred advocacy for the rights of neglected children made a significant change in the lives of *adivasis*.

Both the organisations played an important role in addressing the issues of *adivasis* for freeing them from human bondage, protecting their livelihood, and for providing them with opportunities for education and employment. This impacted the socio-economic and political lives of these *adivasis*.

Picture 4.17: *The children participated in demonstrations for the right to education.*

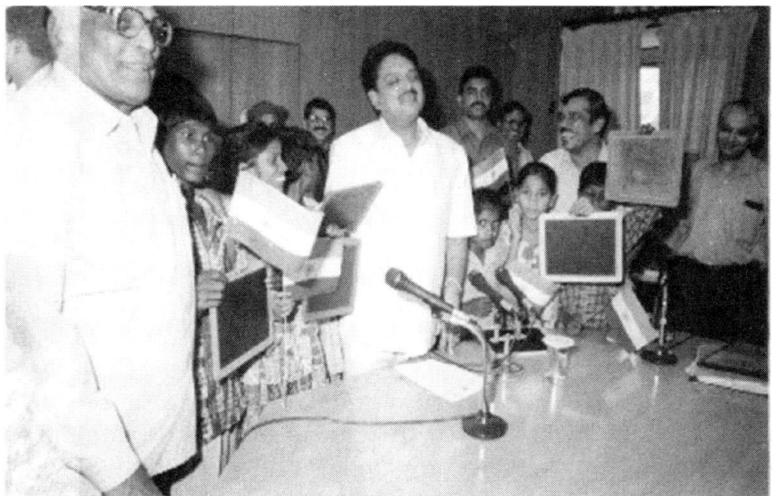

Picture 4.18: *The children with Chief Minister Mr. Vilasrao Deshmukh along with N.D. Patil and Vivek Pandit during the negotiation for the rights to education.*

C. The Campaign for the Right to Work

The organisations advocated and obtained amendments in the Employment Guarantee Scheme, Maharashtra. The author observed that extensive awareness creation had occurred among the members and the people in general. Since the last 30 years, the state government has granted a right to work for the unskilled labourers through the employment guarantee scheme. However, despite the existence of the EGS there was no increase in assets of *adivasis* because the work was carried out on the landholders' land. To enable *adivasis* to create their own assets, the organisations suggested an innovative scheme of plantation.

The section deals with the aspect of the plantation scheme to bringing about an amendment to the EGS scheme.

Through the struggle for the minimum wages and equal wages for men and women, activists created awareness and opportunities for people through the government and organisations' schemes. Initially, the organisations implemented the watershed development programme for employment generation. Later on, this became the productive programme for agriculture improvement. Once people realised that it is the responsibility of the government to create employment opportunities for their citizens, they began building pressures on the government by demanding schemes, which were specifically suitable and beneficial for them. In order to protect and conserve the environment and to support constructive employment for the benefit of farmers, activists initiated the Jatropa plantation movement all over the district. They demanded changes in the EGS schemes because they wanted to promote the plantation of Jatropa (for bio-diesel). As usual, the government was reluctant to incorporate the budget for Jatropa plantation through the EGS, but after the struggle launched both by the Vidhayak Sansad and the Shramjeevi Sanghatana, the government was forced to pay attention and the Department of Agriculture and Food, Government of Maharashtra, issued a Government Resolution on April 23, 2006 (see Appendix p. 179).[15] As a result, as many as 8,500 farmers in Thane district planted more than 35 lakh plants.[16]

For the implementation of this programme, activists took up the Jatropa Campaign in the district with overwhelming support of people's representatives, government offices, and people at large from June 23, 2006.[17] The members of the Shramjeevi Sanghatana had protected and conserved their forest as their lifeline. To conserve it, they agreed to plant trees on their farm *bunds* and barren lands. Because of this initiative they received employment, free plants, nurturing compensation and yields. For the implementation of the scheme, the Shramjeevi Sanghatana organised various block-wise *morchas*, *satyagrahas*, and meetings with ministers, media persons and so on. They requested the government, and the government deposited the first instalment of Rs. 1 crore 22 lakh in favour of Jatropa cultivators in Thane district.[18] All members of the Shramjeevi Sanghatana participated in the campaign of the Jatropa plantation. The author observed that all the members participated in the *Rojgar Yatra* (the march for the right to work) and the Jatropa plantation from the study village.

Picture 4.19: *The women members of the Shramjeevi Sanghatana during the plantation of Jatropa.*

These are the advocacy efforts of the Vidhayak Sansad and the Shramjeevi Sanghatana for the rights of members, in particular and of people, in general. It was observed that most of the members participated in various agitations and celebrations organised by the organisations. The majority of the members benefited through these initiatives of the organisations. Their initiatives brought about changes in their socio-economic and political status. There are many other initiatives for the empowerment of women and children initiated both by the Vidhayak Sansad and the Shramjeevi Sanghatana. The next section, therefore, deals with socio-economic development and empowerment.

5. Social Development and Empowerment

The author analysed the role of organisations in conscientisation, organising, and mobilising, and rights-based advocacy in the previous sections. This section deals with the impact of these initiatives as reflected through the socio-economic and political development and the way towards the empowerment of *adivasis*. The author used the theoretical framework of conscientisation and the concepts of development and empowerment have been discussed in the chapter on research design.

The process of development has been seen on the basis of increase in social well-being, freedom from exploitation and oppression, securing social justice, and bringing about social integration. Social well-being refers to several provisions of social services such as health, education, housing, employment, and social security. It is mostly about getting economic benefits. Freedom from exploitation and oppression of the *adivasis* has been viewed by way of abolition of the practice of bonded labour. Securing social justice involves the practice of equality, preferential allocation and distribution of goods/resources, equality of opportunity, and empowerment. It has been formulated in the interest of Scheduled Castes, Scheduled Tribes, and other disadvantaged and deprived sections of the society.

The process of empowerment is a process of enhancing the ability of powerless individuals/groups aimed at changing the socio-economic and political status of the marginalised, ex-untouchables, *adivasis*, women, and other disadvantaged. In this sense, the term empowerment has been applied for empirical observation in the case of the *adivasi* activists' initiative in the village under study.

The author observed the excellent coordination between the two organisations to achieve the goal of larger social development and change in the lives of the marginalised segments, especially the *adivasis*. Through the process of organising, mobilising, and using rights-based advocacy, the organisations have created a model of development initiatives by civil society for the rights of *adivasis*, which has contributed immensely to set things in bringing social development. The common feature of the organisations can be seen as the important work of bridging the gap between grassroots and state through their people-centred advocacy work.

Through the programmes of socio-economic development such as agriculture development, watershed development, land ownership and sufficient foodgrains for their livelihood, educational programmes for the children, awareness about rights, release and rehabilitation of bonded labourers and policy level changes in employment generation programmes, members were able to attain an enhanced quality of life. Similarly, ensuring effective implementation of the government's programmes resulted in raising the standard of living of the *adivasis* and making them fearless vis-a-vis the oppressive powers.

It was observed that more than 95% of the members participated in the organisations' programmes and benefited. They not only benefited in terms of livelihood but also politically. The process of empowerment is reflected in their decision-making abilities at different levels. Women members of the Shramjeevi Sanghatana were able to become people's representatives in Thane and Nashik districts. During the time of the survey, Mrs. Ambapure, a member of the Shramjeevi Sanghatana was a member of the Panchayat Samiti in the Trimbak block of Nashik.

This chapter aimed at presenting the role of the Vidhayak Sansad and the Shramjeevi Sanghatana in conscientising the *adivasis* and its impact on the members of the organisations. The strategies of organising and mobilising, developing the leadership for advocacy and lobbying, and empowerment of the members were discussed. These strategies resulted in raising people's enlightenment, increasing their confidence, and leading the way towards the development of independent and autonomous leadership among the *adivasis*.

NOTES

1. Pandit, Vidyullatta: *Ropya Mahostav Visheshank*, Shramjeevi Sanghatana, Thane, October, 2007.
2. Reporter: Virarmadhil Pach Vethbeegaranchi Sutka Vidhayak Sansadchaya Karyakartyanche Koutukaspad Karya, *Sakal*, October 14, 1982, Mumbai.
3. Goswami, Paromita: *Taking Roots-Spreading Wings*, Vidhayak Sansad and Shramjeevi Sanghatana, Thane, October 20, 1996, p. 5.
4. Reporter: Vethbeegar Samssenchi Pahani, *Maharashtra Times*, July 13, 1984.
5. Pandit, Vivek: *Fearless Minds*, National Centre for Advocacy Studies, Pune, September 2000, p. 46.
6. Bhoir, Balaram: *Chitramay Itihas Shramjeevi Sanghatana, 1982-2007*, Shramjeevi Sanghatana, Thane, October 21, 2007.

7. Pandit, Vivek: *Fearless Minds*, National Centre for Advocacy Studies, Pune, September, 2000, p. 168.
8. Pandit, Vidyullata: *Annual Report, 2006-2007*,Vidhayak, Sansad, Usgaon Dongari, Thane, 2007, p. 3.
9. Bhoir, Balaram: *Annual Report, 2005-2006*, Shramjeevi Sanghatana, Usgaon Dongari, Thane, 2007, p. 12.
10. Mahajan, Kavita: *Parivartnachaya Prakriyecha Jeetajagata Purava*, Vidhayak Sansad and Shramjeevi Sanghatana, Thane, 1998, p. 8.

5

Conscientisation and Development

1. Recapitulation

In the first chapter, the author discussed the failures of the state machinery in implementing the policies and schemes meant for the welfare of poor and deprived people, especially the socio-economically backward and neglected communities. Various government reports listed these failures and acknowledged the significant role of voluntary organisations as change makers.

During the Emergency (1975), many organisations were formed to protest against the Emergency and to work for the oppressed communities. The Government of India enacted the Foreign Contribution Regulation Act, 1976 to enable the voluntary sector in the country, and gave permission to NGOs to accept foreign money for the development of the marginalised communities so as to work hand in hand with the government for implementing welfare programmes and schemes. The emergence of voluntary organisations or NGOs was recognised by the Government of India which made a separate policy named the *National Policy on the Voluntary Sector, May 2007*.[1] The preamble of the policy states that: "The voluntary sector has contributed significantly to finding innovative solutions to poverty, deprivation, discrimination and exclusion, through means such as awareness raising, social mobilisation, service delivery, training, research and advocacy". Therefore, the policy is a commitment to encourage, enable and empower the voluntary sector so that it would contribute to social, cultural, and economic development of the people of India.

The organisations selected by the author for the current study are active voluntary organisations that have a unique twin model of development using rights-based organising and development intervention along with an integrated perspective towards people's participation and grassroots leadership. As noted, the Shramjeevi Sanghatana is a trade union helping people to assert their rights while the Vidhayak Sansad is the grassroots organisation involved in creating an enabling environment for the empowerment of people. To understand the role of these organisations in conscientisation strategies, rights-based organising, mobilising people to assert their rights, and making people aware about impacts of macro policy, the author examined the specified objectives and tested hypotheses.

In the second chapter, the author discussed the socio-economic condition of the members before and after joining the organisations. The author found that prior to interventions, members were socio-economically dispossessed, neglected from the purview of the state-sponsored development, and were caught in bondage and slavery. They were mentally unprepared to give up bondage by the moneylenders and landlords. They were illiterate and ignorant of social legislations. Their social relations were limited. They had no communication with the outside world, therefore, their world was only their workplace. This resulted in abject poverty and economic dependence. Often, entire families worked as bonded labourers for generations. In some cases, families in the study block were bonded for more than 40 years. Their lands had been taken away. In the name of forest conservation or businessmen had grabbed their lands.

Paulo Freire had focused on dialogic process, of which the essence of education is a practice of freedom. The organisations used the same methods while upholding the larger principle of liberation to overcome oppression. The organisations worked with members on the basis of cooperation, unity, organisation, and cultural synthesis. Initially, the organisations fought against local power relations at village and hamlet levels. This helped to increase the confidence of members through the spirit of winning, which resulted in strong unity and integration among the people. With the intervention of the Vidhayak Sansad and the Shramjeevi Sanghatana, they realised that they were in bondage and lived as slaves.

The author observed the conscientisation methods that were

constantly used by the Vidhayak Sansad and the Shramjeevi Sanghatana. The organisations used local methods, familiar to members. They also used the philosophy of Dr. Babasaheb Ambedkar, who said, *Tell the slave he is slave and he will revolt.*[2] Thus, they prepared and persuaded members to come out of social slavery and created thousands of fearless minds. Members have become fearless through this process.

The leaders used phase-wise *Saha-Adhayan Shibirs* (collective learning camp). Initially, the members were reluctant to analyse their situation as they felt insecure, but with the efforts of leaders, they opened up to change. The activists in the study area acquired the skill of drafting. They could now file cases of bonded labour for submission to the committees. Every year, the organisations organised 10 to12 *Shibirs*, which helped to develop the members' skills, perspectives, information, and knowledge.

The inception of the Vidhayak Sansad and the Shramjeevi Sanghatana is deeply rooted in the struggle against injustice and getting people's rights. Both the organisations worked with the same people and on the same issues. Their initial goal was to free members from bondage and slavery. The next step was to carry out development interventions for the survival of members. The development interventions of the Vidhayak Sansad focused on eradication of the illegal practices of money-lending in the study area and rehabilitation of the freed bonded labourers with support from the government.

The larger aim of the development programmes was to sustain livelihoods. With the help of new technologies, the organisations helped improve the fertility of lands and thus helped to reduce their burden on the *Khavati* (food consumption loan) programme. A variety of programmes were implemented viz. land levelling, sharecropping, watershed development, fodder collection, developing own brick industry, cooperative societies such as milk cooperative, fishery cooperative, truck cooperative, savings and credit cooperative, Warli art, and several government schemes related to economic development. The combination of development efforts and organising the *adivasi* people made these interventions more sustainable as both aspects are complementary to each other. As the economic aspect of development was incorporated with the awareness of rights and causes of poverty, the effects are more complete and holistic. Some of the changes were direct such as increasing income level, increasing employment, awareness about rights and getting access to secure their rights. Other equally important changes such as decreasing migration and narrowing socio-economic disparity within local social segments were also observed.

Some of the members acquired skills such as driving and a few of them now owned auto rickshaws. Most of the members were observed to be using mobiles to communicate with one another. Earlier, due to not having the experience of organising a union and owing to lack of experience of running cooperatives, some of the unions and cooperatives had to be discontinued. However, with the dual approach used by organisations, members had now become enabled to deal with these issues. Initially, the members used to depend on their leaders, but are now able to make their own decisions.

The author observed significant changes in the lives of *adivasis* due to the conscientisation programmes. The organisations helped to develop faith and self-respect amongst the *adivasis*. It will not be out of place to mention the advice given by Dr. Babasaheb Ambedkar to the socially oppressed people that, *educate, agitate, and organise; have faith in yourself. With justice on our side, I do not see how we can lose the battle.*[3] Every activity had components to enable change in the power relations in society. It was observed that there was a paradigm shift in approaches from welfare to the rights-based approach among the members. to the following section presents the socio-economic, cultural and political changes as follows:

A. Economic Development

In any family or society, the economic condition is considered a crucial factor of development. A significant difference in situations before and after the interventions of the organisations was observed as noted in previous chapters. Among various factors, the author observed the housing condition of members, and found that 98% now had their own homes. Members shared that owning their homes was a great achievement in their lives.

Another important factor was that the entitlement of the house was often in the woman's name. Thus, 20% of the women members had their names on the property records. As many as 92% of members had connectivity of electricity and had access to potable water in the study hamlets.

It was also seen that a majority of the members had their own livestock. Also, it was observed that the number of livestock animals had increased. In the study area, it was found that all the members had sufficient food grains for annual consumption. Almost all the members had houses with two rooms. Most of the members had *pucca* houses built with modern material. Similarly, before the interventions of organisations, members did not hold any kind of land assets, but with the help of organisations, many of them were able to reclaim and regularise their land entitlements. Some of the members had joint land entitlement on their land records and house records.

There was a shift in the employment and occupation pattern as well. Members were now engaged in agriculture and allied activities. Parents of the current members were either bonded labourers or agricultural labourers who had to migrate in search of work. In the current scenario, migration was seen to have reduced markedly due to the availability of employment in the village. Now, a large majority of the members were seen to be cultivating their own lands. Almost 94% of the respondents owned land. This indicates a significant change in their livelihood and food security pattern. A majority (75%) had annual yield between six and twelve quintals. Incomes have risen by Rs. 1,000 to Rs 3,000. Earlier members were indebted to moneylenders and landlords. With increased incomes they are now able to save money which they do by forming SHGs or depositing savings in local banks (see Appendix p. 178). In the current scenario, members were both able to and eager to educate the next generation. The next part deals with the social development of the *adivasis*.

B. Social Development

Social development is an important factor in the life of every human being. The education of members and their social relations are the crucial components of social development. The author observed a shift from illiteracy to literacy in *adivasi* families in the study area. Ways of thinking and attitudes have changed and they now realise the importance of education.

Previously, the children of the respondents worked as child labourers, particularly in brick-kilns and agriculture, while some looked after younger siblings. However, after intervention of the organisations, children from the community began to attend school regularly. In order to propagate school education among the *adivasis,* organisations initiated innovative but appropriate programmes such as the *Bhonga Shala, Mukta Shala, Shibir Shala, Ekalavya Shala, Vasti Shala, Study Classes,* and *Bal Sanghatana.* These were later made independent and were now headed and run by the ex-bonded labourers. Both the organisations made special efforts to develop interest in education for the members' children. They were also able to influence the mainstream school system through their educational programmes. They later obtained government permission and grants to manage schools where the government has not yet reached. Additionally, the Tribal Development Commissioner made a special provision for the *adivasi* children to help them in providing educational facilities. With the help of this provision, children of members and others were able to complete their graduation. Some of these graduates were now teachers in primary schools.

Awareness about education and health increased among the members in the study area. Earlier, malnutrition and hunger was rampant due to the absence of food security and health services. Ignorance of health issues and a lack of knowledge about family planning methods also prevailed. Post-intervention, some of the members became *Pada Arogya Rakshak* (hamlet health workers). This resulted in increasing the age at marriage and childbirth. Earlier the girls were married immediately after attaining puberty, but now, child marriages were no longer the norm in the study area.. The author observed that more than 75% of the families were aware about the legal age of marriage.

Though the area is characterised by a majority of *adivasi* population, in the past, there were many social restrictions on the *Katkari* and *Ma Thakur adivasis.* This was no longer the case. Now, different tribes freely mingled socially and shared meals on social occasions. Different groups also fetched water from the same source and jointly participated in village festivals. Cordial relations across different communities were the norm. Collective celebration of traditional festivals by all groups was seen. Importantly, the behaviour of shopkeepers, moneylenders, and landlords towards *adivasis* changed for the better. Thus, collective participation in every programme resulted in unity and strength of *adivasis*.

The author observed that women members were at the forefront in all programmes, including protests, training, and participation in decision-making at different levels. Interestingly, all women members go to the weekly market and decide which items should be bought. Members' relations not only developed among the *adivasis* but also with non-*adivasis* and government officials.

C. Cultural Development

The organisations also paid adequate attention towards the preservation of *adivasi* art and folk culture. The folk culture is not only a means of entertainment but it is also a way of life. The organisations have used cultural forms of the community as a tool of awareness, organising and mobilising the *adivasis* on several issues. Songs such as *Waghya, Chedoba, Himai, Hirwa* and *Palghatdevi,* which feature the popular deities of *adivasis* were included by the organisations in their programmes. Thus, folk-dance competitions were held in each block after harvesting of crops in keeping with the local customs and traditions. These popular songs were also used during protests. The author participated in many cultural programmes and observed that such activities helped inculcate a spirit of unity and integration.

In order to preserve and propagate Warli art, a special Warli Art Gallery was created. Additionally exhibitions in different cities, including Mumbai, Pune and Delhi, were organised. At the time of the study, a freed bonded labourer was the head of the Warli Art Gallery. The gallery had a team of four members who are experts in drawing Warli pictures. The head, late Dama Desak, initiated training programmes so that youth from the community were able to keep alive their traditional heritage (see Appendix pp. 175-177).

With increased socio-cultural and political consciousness, members were now becoming an active part of representative democratic spaces in the local self-government. Therefore, the following part is focused on the political achievement and the way towards the autonomous leadership.

D. Political Development

People's participation in local self-government is an opportunity for the deprived sections of the society. The 73rd amendment to the Constitution has created these spaces and opportunities. Despite the opportunity socio-economically backward people were unable to be a part of the political process. The author observed that through training programmes and political awareness creation, the members were empowered to engage in meaningful participation in local self-government. In every taluka, the members of the Shramjeevi Sanghatana contested election and won under the panel of the Shramjeevi Sanghatana. All members also had their names in the voters list.

In 2005, members contested local elections and more than 35 women members became the Gram Panchayat *Sarpanches* in Thane district. The study village had one such woman *Sarpanch.* A woman, who was a freed bonded labourer, became a member of the Thane Zilla Parishad. Such changes happened not only in Thane district but in Nashik district as well. The Shramjeevi Sanghatana extended conditional support to different political parties during the election based on particulars in the manifesto of political parties. Though the ex-leaders of the Shramjeevi Sanghatana contested elections with the help of political parties, the organisations were careful to not have a long-term association with any political party and would support a political party on the condition that it protected the members' interest. Members of the Sanghatana made people aware about engaging the government machinery for greater transparency and accountability. These dynamics in elections changed the power relations in society.

All the above-mentioned changes occurred owing to the interventions of the organisations in the field of socio-economic, cultural, and political development. Members are helping to strengthen the democratic institutions through the different processes. These organisations proved that policies are not only enough for the betterment of the weaker sections but there must be a proactive policy framework and proactive bureaucracy support to implement policies and schemes. Thus, they could develop a better democratic environment in the lives of disadvantaged *adivasis* in Thane district.

Thus, the major findings could be stated as follows:

1. The enlightenment of the *adivasis* resulted in making them fearless and assertive of their rights to development.
2. The commitment of the leaders and activists to the cause of emancipation developed the spirit of a 'we feeling' and integration among the oppressed people to resist any injustice or oppression.
3. The twin model of organising and development work resulted in empowerment of the *adivasis*.
4. Both organisations helped to release as many as 1,500 bonded labourers. The leaders received the Anti-Slavery award for their work of release and rehabilitation of the bonded labourers.
5. The organisations' efforts resulted in building a rights-based organisation and in influencing government policies and their implementation.
6. The developmental initiatives helped in social development issues such as school education of members' children, knowledge of nutrition and health, training in farming and in using the HYV methods in agriculture, training in setting up cooperatives, watershed development, and so on.
7. With the efforts of the organisations, more than 25,000 members benefited from socio-economic programmes and most of the members now had housing, land holding, and other assets.
8. The changes in entitlement of the assets resulted in having houses and land in the name of women in many cases.
9. The educative role of organisations was instrumental in building the autonomous leadership among the *adivasis*.
10. The freed bonded labourers now headed various departments in the organisations and they had also

become the president of the organisations.

11. The leadership development programmes and strategies of organising resulted in developing leadership qualities of risk-taking, negotiating with government officers, organising protests, and giving speeches to large masses among the members.
12. The schooling programme resulted in bringing a large number of children into the education stream.
13. The members' active participation in political process resulted in positioning the members to become *Sarpanch* of the Gram Panchayat, the members of Panchayat Samiti, and the members of the Zilla Parishad.
14. The organisations developed a proactive relationship with the legislators, bureaucrats, and media. This resulted in better implementation of the schemes, exclusively for the *adivasis* in the study area.
15. The work in partnership with government in the field of education, employment, and health resulted in greater implementation of the schemes.
16. With the intervention of both the organisations, all the members in the study area got their lands regularised.
17. The role of advocacy and lobbying resulted in a pro-policy environment of education and employment for the *adivasis*.

2. Discussion and Conclusion

The objective of the study was to examine the role of conscientisation of the select voluntary organisations in the development of the *adivasis* in Thane district and to observe the impact on the members of the organisations in making governance accountable and transparent. The thrust of the study was conscientisation of *adivasis* by the organisations through their educative role, which resulted in the emergence of autonomous leadership among the *adivasis*. The role of the organisations in breaking the *culture of silence* of the marginalised is based on the method of Paulo Freire.[4] Unless and until people realise their ignorance and lethargy, and the situation of economic, social and political domination, within which they become victims, they cannot bring about a beneficial change.

Both the organisations took tremendous efforts to make members realise their condition of slavery and their poverty using pedagogical methods. As the organisations had a strong ideological base (of Mahatma Gandhi, Dr. Babasaheb Ambedkar, Jayaprakash Narayan, Martin Luther King Jr, Sane Guruji, and S.M. Joshi), it helped in building a strong commitment and efforts by the activists to reduce the injustice and oppression in the lives of the *adivasis*. They strongly believe in *truth and non-violence* and used the various strategies while struggling against the levers of power. In his autobiography, Mahatma Gandhi said that: *I have nothing new to teach the world. Truth and non-violence are as old as the hills.*[5] The organisations used Gandhi's philosophy of organising mass movement for their rights. They used *Satyagraha, Fast, Non-Cooperation* and *Cooperation* and *Civil Disobedience* to strengthen their truth and unity to assert their rights.[6] The organisations used the strategy of socialist S.M. Joshi what he had emphasised: *The only truth in itself is not enough, there has to be strength of Sanghatana.*[7]

The organisations emphasised learning by doing and doing by learning as a principle of learning and sharing of experience by applying the philosophy of Dr. Babasaheb Ambedkar who gave the slogan to his people: *Educate, Agitate and Organise.*[8] This helped creating a spirit of organisation.

Thus, the broad vision and ideas of the organisations resulted in perspective building of the *adivasis*. The study of Vidhayak Sansad and the Shramjeevi Sanghatana revealed the empowerment method of development. The organisations employed a two-pronged strategy of development: 1) organising and mobilising the people through the approach of conscientisation and campaigns; 2) framing of issues and articulating of their demands and drawing the attention of government towards these issues for better implementation for the benefits of the people. The Vidhayak Sansad and the Shramjeevi Sanghatana have had various victories, including the release and rehabilitation of bonded labourers, reclaiming the land rights, change in educational policy and support to innovative schooling programmes for the *adivasis* in the district, necessary amendments to the rural employment scheme, etc.

Both the organisations' struggle at grassroots level along

with policy level interventions helped thousands of *adivasi* families and landless labourers to lead meaningful lives with dignity. In the journey of the organisations, they developed several institutions of activism and advocacy for securing rights and justice. The socio-political and economic empowerment has been the key for reduction of poverty, removing injustice and bringing about overall development.

The way of freedom from fear, ignorance, and humiliation, was given by Gurudev Rabindranath Tagore in his *Gitanjali* poem:

> *Where the mind is without fear and the head is held high;*
> *Where knowledge is free;*
> *Where the world has not been broken up into fragments of narrow domestic walls;*
> *Where the words come out from the depth of truth;*
> *Where tireless striving stretches its arms towards perfection;*
> *Where the clear stream of reason has not lost its way into the*
> *Dreary desert sand of dead habit;*
> *Where the mind is lead forward by thee into ever-widening thought and action;*
> *Into that heaven of freedom, my father, let my country awake.*[9]

In other words, every person has to live with dignity, and strive for truth and perfection.

The father of the nation, Mahatma Gandhi, said that when the last person of the society becomes able and fearless, that is the success of democracy.

Both the organisations use the value *cooperate whenever is possible and resist where it is must*. These fundamental values and strong commitment to the cause of the *adivasi* people have resulted in rights-based development and empowerment. Leadership development among the *adivasis* was the effective way towards the emergence of autonomous leadership and which is the real sign of independence. People have become fearless and are able to ask questions to the concerned decision-makers for their rights.

Thus, both primary and secondary data confirm the hypothesis that the emergence of the voluntary organisations resulted in bringing about the overall development of *adivasis* and better cooperation and collaboration with government in implementing programmes. Thus, the role of voluntary organisations in conscientisation, organising, and mobilising the *adivasis* and a programme for the people-centred advocacy has been instrumental in making the government machinery pro-poor by implementing development programmes with greater transparency and accountability. It is important to note that the government entrusted various development programmes to Panchayati Raj institutions and to voluntary organisations. The Patil Committee specifically stated that general education, welfare of women and children, and primary health services are the areas where participation of voluntary organisations could be encouraged.[10]

The development initiatives by the Vidhayak Sansad and the Shramjeevi Sanghatana resulted in freedom from fear, assertion of rights, and the improvement of relations in society. The efforts made for eradicating human bondage and bringing about socio-economic change along with dignity, justice, and fearlessness demonstrate that true development can be achieved only when people are awakened and are empowered to end injustice and oppression. The study concludes that the ideological base of the founders of the organisations made the *adivasis* autonomous, independent, and self-supportive and altered their status of servitude through initiating and accomplishing the task of conscientisation.

NOTES

1. Government of India: *National Policy on the Voluntary Sector*, Planning Commission, May, 2007, p. 1.
2. Keer, Dhananjay: *Dr. Babasaheb Ambedkar (Marathi Biography)*, Popular Prakashan, Mumbai, 2006, p. 67.

   * It was the slogan of the organisation *Bahishkrit Hitkarini Sabha* (the association of the welfare of untouchables) founded by Dr. Babasaheb Ambedkar in 1924.
3. Kaushik, Pitambar Datt: Ambedkar-Prophet of Self-Help and Saviour of Untouchables, in *Bhimrao Ramji Ambedkar: A Biography of His Vision and Ideas*, edited by Grover, Verinder, Deep & Deep Publications, New Delhi, 1998, p. 252.
4. Freire, Paulo: *Pedagogy of the Oppressed*, Penguin, Harmondsworth, 1996, p. 15.

5. Gandhi, M.K.: *An Autobiography or The Story of My Experiments with Truth*, Navajivan Publishing House, Ahmedabad, April, 2001.
6. Mukherjee, Rudrangshu: *The Penguin Gandhi Reader*, Penguin Books, New Delhi, 1993.
7. Pandit, Vidyullata: *Shramjeevi Sanghatana Annual Report-2003*, Shramjeevi Sanghatana, Thane, 2004.
8. Vakil, A.K.: Political Socialisation of Scheduled Castes and Dr. Ambedkar, in *Bhimrao Ramji Ambedkar: A Biography of His Vision and Ideas*, edited by Grover, Verinder, Deep & Deep Publications, New Delhi, 1998, p. 178.
9. Tagore, Rabindranath: *Gitanjali*, Full Circle Publishing (A Division of Hind Pocket Books Pvt. Ltd.), Delhi, 2002, p. 51.
10. Government of India: *Maharashtra Development Report*, Planning Commission, Government of India, Academic Foundation, New Delhi, 2007, p. 294.

Appendices

1. Campaign for the Release of Bonded Labourers from Thane District
2. Developmental Programmes for the Freedom of Bonded Labourers
3. Members' Saving Accounts and Joint Property Records
4. Advocacy Efforts for Policy Change

APPENDIX I: CAMPAIGN FOR THE RELEASE OF BONDED LABOURERS FROM THANE DISTRICT

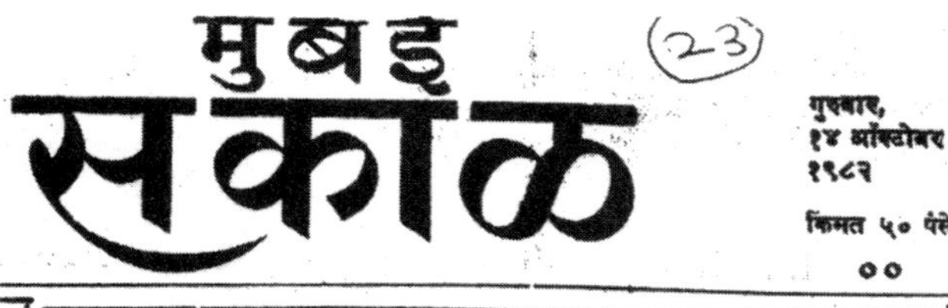

मुंबई सकाळ

गुरुवार, १४ ऑक्टोबर १९८२

किंमत ५० पैसे

[illegible]

विरारमधील पाच वेठबिगारांची सुटका

विधायक संसद कार्यकर्त्यांचे कौतुकास्पद कार्य

(आमच्या प्रतिनिधीकडून)

मुंबई, ता. १३– मुंबईपासून अवघ्या ८० कि. मी. वर विरारपासून १३ कि. मी. अंतरावर असणाऱ्या दहिसर खेड्यातील पाच वेठबिगारांची आज अधिकृत मुक्तता करण्यात आली आणि त्यांना एकूण १२,८८४ ची थकबाकी कामगार उपायुक्त ठाणे यांच्या कार्यालयात मिळवून देण्यात आली. याच खेड्यातील तीन वेठबिगारांना रु. दहा हजारांची थकबाकी १७ ऑगस्ट रोजी विधायक संसदेने मिळवून दिली होती.

'मुंबई सकाळ'नेच सर्वप्रथम हे प्रकरण उघडकीस आणले होते.

वेठबिगारांची कहाणी

दहिसर खेड्यातील श्री. वामन केशव पाटील यांच्याकडे परंपरेने वेठबिगारी पद्धत चालत होती. त्यांच्याकडे नारायण केशव पिलाना यांनी ३० वर्षे वसंत शिडू किरकिरा यांनी २५ वर्षे, अशोक पांडू कामडी यांनी १० वर्षे तर मनोहर गोवर परेड यांनी १॥ वर्षे, श्रीमती येसुबाई धोंडो पाटील यांच्याकडे विष्णू चेंद्या किरकिरा यांनी २५ वर्षे चाकरी केली होती. वयाच्या तेराव्या–चौदाव्या वर्षी ते धन्याकडे गुरे-बकऱ्या सांभाळण्यापासून सुरुवात करीत हळूहळू घरकामे शेतीची कामे करीत, मात्र लग्नासाठी कर्ज मिळे, ३ साड्या, ३ चोळ्या, ५ मण भात, मीठ मसाला सदरा लेंगा आदी पाचशे रुपयेपर्यंतचे त्या बदल्यात यांनी आयुष्यभर राबायचे, मजुरी मिळणार फक्त वर्षाला १५ मण भात, १ घोंगडी, २ रुमाल.

विधायक संसदने तहसीलदार वसई यांच्याकडे १२ मे ८२ रोजी सदर तक्रारी केल्या होत्या. तहसीलदारांना अधिकार नसल्याने त्या तशाच तेथे पडून राहिल्या. अखेर संघटनेच्या बळावर हा प्रश्न सोडविण्यात यश आले. या करारावर श्रमजीवी संघटनेतर्फे अध्यक्ष विवेक पंडित, कार्याध्यक्ष विद्युल्लता पंडित व जन. सेक्रेटरी प्रभाकर लकेश्री यांनी सह्या केल्या. मालकातर्फे श्री. वामन केशव पाटील व प्रतिनिधी सुरेश शिपन्या भोईर यांच्या सह्या झाल्या. कामगार उपायुक्त श्री. निकुंभ यांच्या समक्ष हा करार झाला. सहाय्यक आयुक्त श्री. वि. बा. सावंत यांच्यासमोर चर्चा झाली.

गुरुवारीस विधायक संसदने या प्रश्नाला वाचा फोडली, आता विधायक संसदने आदिवासी शेतमजूर, भूमिहीन आणि अल्पभूधारक शेतकऱ्यांची "श्रमजीवी संघटना" "श्रमिक संघटना" निर्माण केली आहे. जमीनदार आणि प्रस्थापितांच्या दडपणामुळे हे वेठबिगार पुढे येत नव्हते, परंतु आत्मविश्वास जागृत केल्यानंतर हा प्रश्न सुटला. दहिसर परिसरात अजून कितीतरी वेठबिगार आहेत, श्रमजीवी संघटना आता आपले लक्ष या कामीच केंद्रीत करीत आहे.

शेतमजुरांचा संप

दहिसर खेड्यात फक्त तीन रुपये व एक जेवण एवढीच मजुरी मिळते. ती पाच रुपये व एक जेवण मिळावे यासाठी पंधरा दिवस दहिसरमधील मजूरांनी संप पुकारला असून काही जमीन मालकांनी त्याप्रमाणे मजुरी देण्यास सुरुवात केली आहे. जे देणार नाहीत त्यांच्या शेताची कापणी न करण्याचा शेतमजुरांचा निर्धार आहे. श्री. चण्णा भोवर व श्री. पांडुरंग भोईर हे संघटक यासाठी विशेष प्रयत्नशील आहेत

News clip 1: Release of five bonded labourers from the Vasai block in Thane district. The news was published in *Mumbai Sakal*, October 14, 1982.

महाराष्ट्र टाइम्स

वर्ष २१ : अंक ६० मुंबई, बुधवार, १८ ऑगस्ट १९८२

साडीचोळी, ५ मण भातासाठी २२ वर्षे वेठबिगारी

(आमच्या प्रतिनिधीकडून)

मुंबई, मंगळवार — २ लुगडी, २ चोळ्या, सदरा, साधे मणीमंगळसूत्र, धोतर आणि ५ मण भात यांची किंमत किती? पैशात या वस्तूंची किंमत कितीही असो, पण श्रमात मात्र या वस्तू बाळू धागड्या किरकिरा याला [illegible] वर्षांना पडल्या, तब्बल २२ वर्षांना!

बाळूने लग्नासाठी या वस्तू सावकाराकडून घेतल्या आणि या वस्तूंची किंमत फेडण्यासाठी सावकाराकडे त्याला २२ वर्षे अन्नासाठी राबावे लागले. वेठबिगारी नष्ट करणारा कायदा संमत होऊनही असे अनेक बाळू वेठबिगारीवर घाम गाळीत आहेत.

वेठबिगारीस प्रतिबंध करणारा कायदा केन्द्र सरकारने सहा वर्षांपूर्वी संमत केला, परंतु त्याची अंमलबजावणी करता यावी याकरिता राज्य सरकारने संबंधित प्रशासकांना अधिकार देण्याची व्यवस्था अजून केलेली नसल्याचा विधायक संसद या संस्थेचा अनुभव आहे.

स्थानिक अधिकाऱ्यांना या कायद्यानुसार अजून अधिकार मिळाले नसल्याने आता फार तर अशा वेठबिगार कामगारांची सावकाराच्या कचाट्यातून फक्त मुक्तता होते. परंतु अनेक वर्षे त्यांच्याकडून करून घेतलेल्या कामाबद्दलचा मोबदला मात्र त्यास मिळत नाही.

दहिसरमधील घटना

विरारजवळच्या दहिसर गावातील (ठाणे जिल्हा) एका सावकाराकडे वेठबिगारांचे तीन गडी असल्याचे विधायक संसदेचे कार्यकर्ते श्री. विवेक पंडित आणि श्रीमती विद्युल्लता वि. पंडित यांना कळल्याने त्यांनी हे प्रकरण हाती घेतले. या गड्यांपैकी बाळू धागड्या किरकिरा हा तर २२ वर्षे सावकाराकडे अगदी फुकट दिवसभर कष्ट उपसत होता.

लग्नासाठी सावकाराकडून कर्ज घेतल्याने ते वेठबिगारीच्या कचाट्यात सापडले. आणि हे कर्ज तरी किती मोठे? फक्त २ लुगडी, २ चोळ्या, एक सदरा-धोतर, अथवा लंगोट, ५ मण भात, लग्न समारंभानंतरच्या जेवणावळीसाठी लागणारा मीठमसाला, थोडा शेव-चिवडा आणि एक साधे मंगळसूत्र. या साऱ्या साहित्याची किंमत हजार रुपये सावकार धरतो.

या कर्जाची परतफेड वर्षास शंभर रुपयांच्या हप्त्याने करावयाची असते. याचा अर्थ त्या कामगाराने वर्षभर सावकाराकडे काम केले तरच हा हप्ता भरला असे धरले जात असे. त्याला या श्रमाबद्दल वर्षाकाठी १५ मण भात, १ घोंगडी आणि कमरेभोवती बांधावयाचे दोन रुमाल एवढाच मोबदला दिला जात आहे. अशा प्रकारे मूळ कर्जाची भरपाई करण्यासाठी १० वर्षे, त्याच्या व्याजाबद्दल २ वर्षे आणि अधूनमधून या बारा वर्षांत केलेल्या खाड्याबद्दल आणखी एक वर्ष मिळून तेरा वर्षे लग्न-कर्जापोटी या गड्यांना राबवून घेण्याची ही प्रथा.

विधायक संसदने दहिसर येथील या तीन वेठबिगार गड्यांचे प्रकरण हाती घेतल्यावर संबंधित सावकाराकडे त्यांनी अनेक वर्षे केलेल्या कामाचे वेतन म्हणून २४,६०० रुपयांची मागणी केली होती. कारण हे गडी अनुक्रमे २२, १४ व ७ वर्षे सावकाराकडे लग्न-कर्जापायी अगदी फुकट राबत होते. शेवटी त्यासंबंधी समझोता होऊन या तीन श्रमिकांना एकूण दहा हजार रुपये देण्याचे सावकाराने मान्य केल्याचे — तसा करार केल्याचे श्री. पंडित यांनी सांगितले.

News clip 2: The leaders of the Vidhayak Sansad and Shramjeevi Sanghatana released three bonded labourers in village Dahisar in Vasai block. The three bonded labourers were caught in slavery for more than 22 years in the block. This news appeared in *Maharashtra Times* on August 18, 1982.

महाराष्ट्र टाइम्स

वर्ष २३ : अंक ११ मुंबई, शुक्रवार, १३ जुलै १९८४ ५५ पैसे

वेठबिगार समस्येची पाहणी

चौकशी समितीची वसई तालुक्यास अभ्यास-भेट

(आमच्या प्रतिनिधीकडून)

वेठबिगारमुक्त आदिवासी चरितार्थास लागले

(आमच्या प्रतिनिधीकडून)

News clip 3: The Enquiry Committee appointed by Hon. Supreme Court to investigate the condition of the bonded labourers in Thane district. The committee members were Dr. Satyaranjan Sathe and Dr. Vasudha Dhagamwar. The news was reflected in *Maharashtra Times* on July 13, 1984.

वसई तालुक्यात चार पिढ्या वेठबिगारी करणाऱ्या २३ वेठबिगारांची मुक्तता

(आमच्या प्रतिनिधीकडून)

ठाणे, ता. १८–वसई तालुक्यातील मांडवी गावातील भगवान शिवराम देसाई यांच्याकडे चार पिढ्या काम करणाऱ्या आठ कुटुंबातील २३ वेठबिगारांची सुटका श्रमजीवी संघटनेने केली आहे. वेठबिगार कायद्याच्या विरोधात भगवान शिवराम देसाई यांच्यावर विरार पोलीस स्टेशनमध्ये गुन्हा दाखल करण्यात आला आहे.

या २३ वेठबिगाऱ्यांच्या मुक्तीचे अर्ज श्रमजीवी संघटनेचे अध्यक्ष विवेक पंडित यांनी जिल्हाधिकारी भास्कर पाटील यांना सादर केले असून त्यांनी योग्य ती कारवाई करण्याचे आदेश वसई तहसीलदारांना दिले आहेत.

चाळीस वर्षे वेठबिगारी

मुक्त झालेल्या वेठबिगाऱ्यांपैकी रामजी ठुंभले याने भगवान देसाई यांच्या आजोबांकडून पाचशे रुपयांचे कर्ज चाळीस वर्षापूर्वी घेतले होते. लग्नापूर्वी बारा वर्षे रामजी काम करीत होता. एकूण ५२ वर्षे झाली तरी रामजीने घेतलेले पाचशे रुपये अजूनही फिटले नाहीत. रामजी आज ६२ वर्षांचा आहे. रोज १२–१३ तास काम करूनही रामजीला आठवड्याला २४ रुपये मिळतात व दोन वर्षातून एकदा घोंगडी मिळते. अशी माहिती देऊन श्रमजीवी संघटनेचे विवेक पंडित यांनी सांगितले की, केशव लक्ष्मण [illegible] हा ५२ वर्षांचा वेठबिगार [illegible] बायको, तीन मुले व दोन सुना यांच्यासह भगवान देसाई यांच्याकडे ४० ते ४२ वर्षे काम करीत आहेत. केशवचे वडील, आई, भाऊ आजोबांपासून भगवान देसाई यांच्याकडे वेठबिगारी करीत आहेत. तसेच चंटया जान्या लोखंडे हा [illegible] लग्नासाठी [illegible] फेडण्यासाठी [illegible] चाळीस वर्षे वेठबिगारी करीत आहे. या वेठबिगाऱ्यांनी १९ सप्टेंबरपासून संप पुकारला व मिळेल तेथे काम करण्याचा प्रयत्न केला तेव्हा भगवानशेठने दमदाटीने त्यांचे कामावर जाणे बंद केले.

४० वर्षांची अंधारयात्रा अखेर संपली

तीन वर्षापूर्वी [illegible] मुक्त – वसई परिसरातील [illegible] वेठबिगार तीन वर्षापूर्वी [illegible] मुक्त केले. पाच महिन्यापूर्वीच भगवान शेठच्या नातेवाईकांकडील १३ वेठबिगार संघटनेने शोधून काढले.

आज मुक्त केलेल्या वेठबिगाऱ्यांची नावे पुढीलप्रमाणे–

(१) रामजी लडक्या चुंबले (वय ६२), त्याची पत्नी रखुमाई (५६).

(२) अनुसया काना चुंबले (५०), भगवान चुंबले (२६), त्याची पत्नी जयवंती (२२), शांताराम (२४), त्याची पत्नी तुळशीबाई (२२).

(३) केशव लक्ष्मण धागड (५२), पत्नी शेवंतीबाई (४५), मुलगा चंदर (२८), पत्नी मजुळा (२५), नाना (२४), पत्नी शारदा (२१), राम [illegible].

(४) [illegible] जैसू धागडा (२७), पत्नी [illegible]बाई (२५).

(५) [illegible] जान्या लोखंडे (५०), पत्नी शकुनबाई (४६).

(६) रमेश जान्या लोखंडे (३०), पत्नी रमाबाई (२५).

(७) सुनिताबाई मंगळ लोखंडे (२७)

(८) किसन गायकर (३०), पत्नी ताईबाई (२५).

तुंबलेले खटले

श्रमजीवी संघटनेचे अध्यक्ष विवेक पंडित यांनी सर्वोच्च न्यायालयात दाखल केलेल्या याचिकेवर महाराष्ट्र शासनाने सर्वोच्च न्यायालयाला खटले लवकरात निकालात काढण्यासाठी प्रतिज्ञापत्र सादर केले आहेत. सप्टेंबर १९८४ पासून आजपर्यंत एकूण चार दंडाधिकारी नियुक्त झाले. परंतु एकही खटला निकालात निघाला नाही. नेमणूक होणारा प्रत्येक दंडाधिकारी एकतर निवृत्त होण्याच्या काळात तरी येतो किंवा अन्य ठिकाणी बदली झाल्यावर तात्पुरत्या स्वरूपात तरी येतो. आज ही जागा रिकामी आहे. सरकारला हे खटले निकालात काढण्याची इच्छा नाही हेच यातून सिद्ध होते. सर्वोच्च न्यायालयाचा महाराष्ट्र सरकारने हा अवमान चालविला आहे याची दाद सर्वोच्च न्यायालयात मागण्याचा श्रमजीवी संघटना विचार करीत आहे असे विवेक पंडित यांनी सांगितले.

News clip 4: The Vidhayak Sansad and Shramjeevi Sanghatana released 23 bonded labourers who were engaged in slavery for the last forty years in Vasai Block district Thane. The news was reflected in the *Mumbai Sakal* on December 19, 1986.

महाराष्ट्र टाइम्स

मुंबई, गुरुवार, २३ एप्रिल १९८७ (भारतीय सौर ३ वैशाख १९०९)

गणेशपुरी आश्रमातील मजुरांची मारहाणीची तक्रार

(आमच्या प्रतिनिधीकडून)

मुम्बई, बुधवार — गणेशपुरी येथील गुरुदेव सिध्दपीठ आश्रमातील परदेशी 'भक्तगणां'नी, आश्रमास 'देणगीवर्ष' राबणाऱ्या स्त्री-पुरुष मजुरांना मारहाण केल्याची तक्रार असून, सोमवारपासून आश्रमातील सुमारे ३०० मजूर संपावर गेले आहेत.

शनिवारी काही मजुरांना मारहाण झाल्यानंतर, रविवारी आश्रमातील सर्व मजूर काम बंद करून बाहेर पडले. परंतु पोलिसांनी मजुरांची तक्रार नोंदवून घेण्याऐवजी त्यांनाच दमदाटी केली. अशी मजुरांची तक्रार आहे.

अखेर सोमवारी 'श्रमजिवी संघटने'तर्फे सिध्दपीठ आश्रमाबाहेर जाहीर सभा घेण्यात आली व मजुरांनी बेमुदत संपावर जाण्याचा निर्णय घेतला.

आश्रमाच्या हॉटेल्समध्ये ४०, बांधकाम प्रकल्पांवर ५४ व उद्यानांच्या देखभालीसाठी सुमारे २०० असे एकूण ३०० मजूर काम करतात. हॉटेलमध्ये काम करणाऱ्या कामगारांत गेली २० ते २५ वर्षे नोकरी झालेले कामगार बहुसंख्य आहेत, असा संघटनेचा दावा आहे.

परंतु या मजुरांना किमान वेतनापेक्षा कमी मजुरी दिली जाते तसेच कायद्याने लागू होणाऱ्या कोणत्याही सुविधा दिल्या जात नाहीत; या मजुरांच्या नोकरीविषयीचे कोणतेही कागदपत्र आश्रम ठेवीत नाही, असा आरोप 'श्रमजिवी संघटने'च्या विद्युल्लता पंडित यांनी केला. मजुरांत आदिवासी व कुणबी जमातीच्या मजुरांचा प्रामुख्याने समावेश आहे.

स्त्री व पुरुष मजुरांना समान वेतन द्यावे, किमान वेतन लागू करावे, अशा मजुरांच्या मागण्या असून जिल्हाधिकारी भास्करराव पाटील व कामगार उप-आयुक्त राम असावेल्ले यांनी मध्यस्थी करावी अशी विनंती संघटनेने केली आहे.

रविवारी निदर्शने

गुरुदेव सिध्दपीठ आश्रमातील 'भक्तगणां'त अनेक मंत्री, शासकीय अधिकारी यांच्यासारख्या उच्चपदस्थांचा समावेश असल्यामुळे मजुरांना न्याय मिळेल की नाही अशी शंका व्यक्त करण्यात येत आहे. मागण्या मान्य न झाल्यास येत्या रविवारी आश्रमासमोर निदर्शने करण्यात येतील असा इशाराही 'श्रमजिवी संघटने'ने दिला आहे.

News clip 5: The campaign against the torture of *adivasis* in Ganeshpuri Aashram. The campaign put demands: minimum wage and equal wages for men and women. The news appeared in *Maharashtra Times* on April 23, 1987.

INDIAN EXPRESS

Bombay: Tuesday December 23 1986

CITY/REGION

Freed.... at last

By Vidya Nayak Root

THE freeing of 23 bonded labourers in Mandvi village of Vasai taluka, about 70 km from Bombay, ended the three-generation-old serfdom that had been imposed on their families. On December 18, eleven couples and one woman all belonging to the Warli Adivasi tribe were freed and a case against the landlord Mr. Babasaheb Mandvikar, was registered by the Virar police.

"It is good to be free. It is good to know that my children and all our future generations will have the choice to do what they want to do," says Rukma Ramji Chumble, who is the oldest woman in the group and has been a bonded labourer for over 40 years. With a slender build and a weather-beaten look, Rukma's face tells a tale of a great deal of hardship. Says she, "Like all the other women here, I was married into bondage. My parents-in-law were bonded labourers with the 'sheth' and consequently so was my husband. So when I got married, I automatically became one.

"I remember we used to get 25 paise a day when I started. I and the other women had to wash dishes, clothes, keep the house clean and then work on the fields as well. We were not allowed to work for anybody else even if it meant we could augment our income. For as long as I remember, the 'sheth' used to cut two days' wages for the loan my husband took for my wedding. It never really occurred to us how this loan never seemed to get cleared.

"I find it hard to believe even now that we are free. I am slowly coming to believe it when I see my sons and the menfolk around going into nearby villages to seek work. It is something we would not have even think of a decade or two ago. Times have changed."

The other women in the group, who are younger, are more vehement in what they have to say about the injustice done to them as also the "mistreatment by the 'sheth'. Sakubai Chaitu Lokhande, says." We had enough of the cruel treatment given to us by the 'sheth'. We were made to work from early in the morning to the late in the evening with hardly any break. The money that was given to us was barely enough for our food. When I married my husband, we used to get Rs. 2 per day. We could almost never make ends meet. So turning to the 'sheth' for a little money as a loan was not out of the ordinary. This poor payment was, of course, a neat ploy to keep us dependent on him. And it worked. For years we were so indebted to him that we did not think of questioning his authority over us. But then the 'sheth' refused to let us work for anybody else. In fact, he went to the extent of asking everybody around that they were not to employ his workers. His influential position in this part made everybody wary of employing us. So we were trapped in every sense."

This "trapped" feeling, the women say, was the reason they started thinking about their plight. "We looked around us and saw that everybody was doing a lot better," says Jayanti Bhagwan Chumble. "We knew then that we would just have to do something," she adds.

That 'something' they did was to approach the Sramajivi Sanghatana, a social organisation based in Dahisar village in Thane district. Ramita Ramesh Lokhande says, "When the 'sheth' found that we had approached the organisation, he was very angry. He tried to dissuade us. But we told him that against the pitiful Rs. 24 a week he was paying us, the market rate for a day's work was between Rs.10 to Rs. 12. There was therefore no question of us staying with him and living poorly."

On being approached by these people, the Sramajivi Sanghatana got in touch with the Thane Collector, Mr. Bhaskarrao Patil who in turn got in touch with the Tehsildar of Vasai Taluka Mr. Shivaji Bahirav. A case was then registered with the Virar police.

Mr. Vivek Pandit President of the Sanghatana claims that nearly 200 bonded labourers in Vasai taluka alone have been freed in the last three years since the Sanghatana started work in this area. In fact the Sanghatana concentrates on detecting cases of bonded labour in Vasai, Vada, Bhiwandi and Shahapur talukas. Since its inception, the Sanghatana has helped free 800 bonded labourers in these districts.

The Collector, Mr. Patil, is quick to admit that implementation of the Bonded Labour Act of 1976 becomes impossible without agencies that can detect the existence of this unlawful activity. He says that it is imperative to have bodies that can inform the authorities about bonded labour cases. The Sramajivi Sanghatana has assisted the authorities of innumerable such cases, he admits.

The acknowlegment of their plight by the governmental bodies has brought a breath of fresh, free air for the 23 people. In fact the men, who have already started working at various jobs in villages, are already happier and better off for it. While a

HAPPY AT LAST: Jayanti, Sakubai and Rukma all smiles o[n] their freedom. (Pic. by Vidya Nayak Root).

number of them have sought field jobs around their home, some of them have taken on construction and brick-laying work in Chandvi, a village nearby.

Says Ramesh Hallya Lokhande, "After 21 years of working for the 'sheth', all I was taking home was a measely Rs. 24 a week. And now, at brick-laying, I earn Rs. 15 a day, which is about Rs. 90 a week. I am glad we finally gathered courage and moved out of that hell-hole.

Shantaram Kana Chumble, who grew up with the 'sheth's three children is quite bitter about how the early years of his life were spent. "Initially, we used to play with the 'sheth's kids. And then there came a time when the 'sheth's kids went off to school in Vasai while we were put to tend buffaloes. Every so often I felt that the buffaloes got a better treatment than we did. In fact the amount spent on feeding and healthcare of the buffalo far exceeded our monthly income.

"Today, with my brick-laying job, with the freedom to do exactly what I want, I am happy, very happy."

His brother Bhagwans Kana Chumble and his friend Ramu Keshav Dhagna have the same story to tell. They are vehement in their feeling that they will never go back to the landlord for. "Even if we starve we will not go back to him," the women say. So what they plan on doing now? "We will take on jobs as and when we get them" they claim. Here c[o]mes the task of rehabilitating th[e] freed from bondage.

This in conjunction with the task [of] identifying bonded labourers [are] probably areas in which the gov[ern]ment has badly let down these peo[ple]. The Bonded Labour clearly st[ates] that once identified, bonded lab[our]ers should be compensated by [the] employer and also rehabilitated [by] the government.

What is holding the smooth im[ple]mentation of this Act is the fact [that] while posts of special executive ma[gis]trates have been created for tr[ying] erring landlords, the posts in mo[st of] the districts are yet to be filled. In[deed] the Collector Mr. Patil, admits th[at this] is one of the most difficult hurdl[es to] cross. "We cannot give them any [kind] of relief until they have been id[enti]fied as bonded labourers," he adm[its]. "The problem is that a numbe[r of] magisterial posts have not been fi[lled]. It makes it impossible for us there[fore] to be of help to even genuine cas[es]."

This problem has been felt so ac[ute]ly that Mr. Vivek Pandit, Preside[nt of] the Sanghtana has filed a petitio[n in] the Supreme Court seeking [an] appropriate writ against the Ma[har]ashtra Government directed it t[o try] cases registered against offen[ding] landlords without delay.

If cases of bonded labourers [are k]ept pending it will surely con[firm w]ith the adage 'justice delaye[d is] justice denied'.

News clip 6: The Vidhayak Sansad and Shramjeevi Sanghatana released 23 bonded labourers from Mandvi village in Vasai block in Thane district. The news appeared in *The Indian Express*, Mumbai on December 23, 1986.

INDIAN EXPRES

WITH EXPRESS MAGAZINE

Bombay: Sunday May 10 1987

Dhundya Jeeper Lathad: "I am glad I am independent"

Dhundya Jeeper Lathad:

Broken bonds

VIDYA NAYAK ROOT reports from Maharashtra on the instance of a landlord being prosecuted for holding a labour bondage.

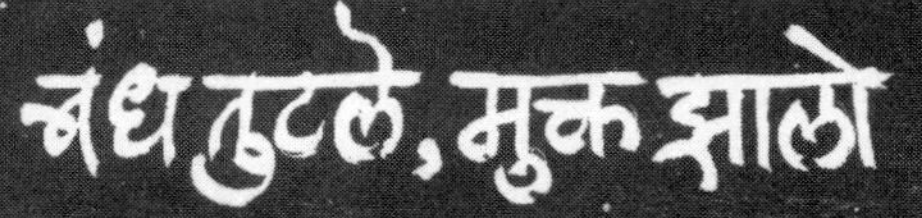

बंध तुटले, मुक्त झालो

News clip 7: The freed bonded labourer with the expression of independence. The news was reflected in *The Indian Express*, Mumbai on May 10, 1987.

APPENDIX II: DEVELOPMENTAL PROGRAMMES FOR THE FREED BONDED LABOURERS

Burudkam (Basket making activity)

Fodder collection

Levelling land for watershed development (Watershed development activity)

Aqua Culture

Schooling Programmes
Vidhayak Sansad Bhonga Shala Project

Schooling activity

Bal Krida Melawa

Annual Bal Melawa at Usgaon

Shramjeevi Sanghatana programmes with people's representatives and executives.

The late Mr. Sandanand Varde, MLA

Meeting with Maharashtra Home Minister, Mr. Chagan Bhujbal at a meeting for strengthening the State Human Rights Commission.

Activists struggle for the Minimum Wages meeting with Tahsildar.

Shramjeevi Sanghatana activists involved in the Killari Earthquake (district Latur) relief work in September 1993.

Rehabilitation project for freed bonded labourers. Painting by the late Dama Desak

Warli Art Gallary

Warli Art Gallary

Warli painting

Warli painting

APPENDIX III: MEMBERS' SAVING ACCOUNTS AND JOINT PROPERTY RECORDS

खाता क्र. A/c. No. 2016689

शाखा / Branch Pelhar

SHREE SAMARTHKRUPA THINAGI MAI

बँक ऑफ महाराष्ट्र

प्र. का. लोकमंगल, शिवाजी नगर, पुणे - ४११ ००५.

बैंक ऑफ महाराष्ट्र

प्र. का. लोकमंगल, शिवाजी नगर, पुणे - 411 005.

बचत खाते पासबुक

बचत खाता पास पुस्तिका

SAVINGS BANK PASS BOOK

BANK OF MAHARASHTRA

H.O. Lokmangal, Shivajinagar, Pune - 411 005.

www.maharashtrabank.com

दिनांक की अनुक्रमांक के अंतर्गत नामांकन पंजीकृत — Nomination Registered On Under Sr. No.

शाखा Branch Pelhar

पत्ता Address AT / PO : TILHER, DHUMALPADA,

दुरध्वनी क्र. Tel. No.

Account No. 2016689	
Account Open Date 13-Jul-2007	**Customer ID** 4837
Account Name	SHREE SAMARTHKRUPA THINAGI MAHILA BACHAT GAT, TILHER
	1) Smt. Rohini Rohidas Mhaskar
	2) Smt. Nikita Nitin Sayare
Mode Of Operation	All Jointly
Nomination	

दिनांक Date — प्राधिकृत अधिकारी Authorised Official

शाखा /Branch

Members' Joint Name on House Property Records

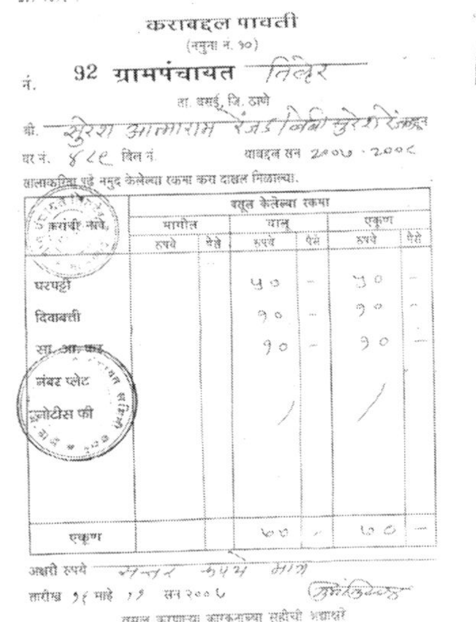

करावद्दल पावती

(नमुना नं. १०)

नं. 92 ग्रामपंचायत तिल्हेर

ता. वसई, जि. ठाणे

श्री. सुरेश आत्माराम

घर नं. ४८८ बिल नं. याबद्दल सन २००७-२००८

सालाकरिता पुढे नमुद केलेल्या रकमा करा दाखल मिळाल्या.

करांची नावे	वसूल केलेल्या रकमा मागील रुपये	पैसे	चालू रुपये	पैसे	एकूण रुपये	पैसे
घरपट्टी			५०	–	५०	–
दिवाबत्ती			१०	–	१०	–
सा. आ. कर			१०	–	१०	–
नंबर प्लेट						
नोटीस फी						
एकूण			७०	–	७०	–

अक्षरी रुपये सत्तर ... मात्र

तारीख १९ माहे १९ सन २००८

वसूल करणाऱ्या कारकुनाच्या सहीची अक्षरे

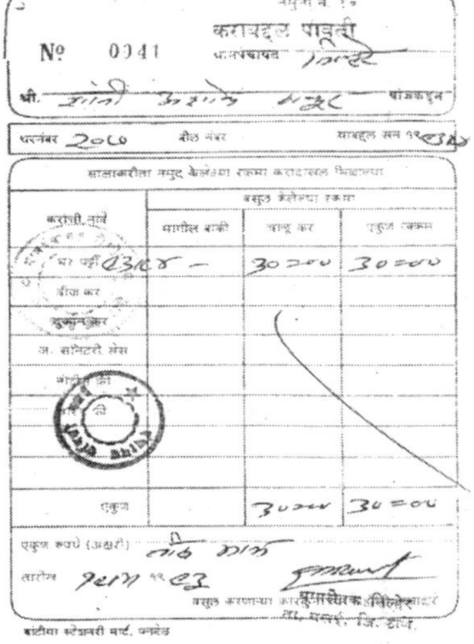

नमुना नं. १०

करावद्दल पावती

№ 0341 ग्रामपंचायत तिल्हेर

श्री.

घरनंबर 200 मील नंबर याबद्दल सन १९८३

सालाकरीता नमुद केलेल्या रकमा कराबद्दल मिळाल्या

करांची नावे	वसूल केलेल्या रकमा मागील बाकी	चालू कर	एकूण रक्कम
घर पट्टी 83-84	–	30=00	30=00
दीवा कर			
अ. सॅनिटरी सेस			
एकूण		30=00	30=00

एकूण रुपये (अक्षरी) तीस मात्र

तारीख

वसूल करणाऱ्या कारकुनाची सही

APPENDIX IV: ADVOCACY EFFORTS FOR THE POLICY CHANGE

Government Resolution on Employment Guarantee Scheme dated 23 April 2006.

G.R.

दहाव्या पंचवार्षिक योजने अंतर्गत रोजगार हमी योजनेशी निगडीत फळझाड लागवडीव्दारे राबविण्यात येत असलेल्या फळविकास योजनेमध्ये सन २००६-०७ मध्ये जट्रोफाचा समावेश करण्याबाबत.

महाराष्ट्र शासन
कृषि, पशुसंवर्धन, दुग्धव्यवसाय विकास व मत्स्यव्यवसाय विभाग,
शासन निर्णय क्रमांक:जट्रोफा-२००५/प्र.क्र.२५३/९-अे
मंत्रालय विस्तार, मुंबई - ४०० ०३२
दिनांक २६ एप्रिल, २००६

वाचा : १) कृषि व पदुम विभाग, शासन निर्णय क्र.रोहयो २००५/प्र.क्र.१/९अे, दि.२७.६.२००५
२) कृषि व पदुम विभाग, शासन निर्णय क्र.अभियान २००५/प्र.क्र.१७१/९अे, दि.२४.११.२००५
३) उद्योग, ऊर्जा व कामगार विभाग, शासन निर्णय क्रमांक:मेडा-२००५/प्र.क्र.२१४८/ ऊर्जा-७, दिनांक ८.१२.२००५

प्रस्तावना :

महाराष्ट्रातील शेतकऱ्यांची आर्थिक प्रगति घडविणे व पडिक जमिनीचा विकास या हेतूने रोजगार हमी योजनेशी निगडीत फळबाग लागवड कार्यक्रम राज्यात सन १९९० पासून राबविण्यात येत आहे. ऊर्जा विभागाने त्यांच्या दिनांक ८.१२.२००५ च्या शासन निर्णयान्वये जाहिर केलेल्या अपारंपारिक ऊर्जा स्त्रोत कार्यक्रम एकत्रित धोरणामध्ये जट्रोफाची लागवड रोजगार हमी योजना फलोत्पादन या योजनेतून करण्याचा निर्णय घेतला आहे. या निर्णयाच्या आधारे जट्रोफा लागवडीकरिता खर्चाची प्रमाणके निश्चित करणे,लागवडीची मर्यादा ठरविणे, लागवडीच्या अनुषंगाने इतर निकष ठरविणे इ.बाबी शासनाच्या विचाराधीन होती.

<u>शासन निर्णय</u> -

दहाव्या पंचवार्षिक योजनेंतर्गत रोजगार हमी योजनेशी निगडीत फळबाग लागवडीव्दारे राबविण्यात येत असलेल्या फळविकास योजनेमध्ये सन २००६-०७ पासून जट्रोफाचा समावेश करण्यास शासनाची मान्यता देण्यात येत आहे.

२. <u>उद्दीष्ट</u> :

सन २००६-०७ मध्ये (प्रथम वर्षी) राज्यात या योजनेअंतर्गत १,११,१०,००० (एक कोटी अकरा लाख दहा हजार) जट्रोफा झाडांची लागवड प्रायोगिक तत्वावर करण्याचे उद्दीष्ट आहे. प्रत्येक जिल्ह्यात जास्तीत जास्त ११,११,००० (अकरा लाख अकरा हजार) जट्रोफा झाडांची लागवड करता येईल. सदर उद्दीष्ट साध्य करण्यासाठी आवश्यक असलेली कलमे/रोपे शासकीय रोपवाटीका, कृषि विद्यापीठ रोपवाटीका, शेती महामंडळ, कृषि विज्ञान केंद्र व राज्यातील खाजगी रोपवाटीकेकडून उपलब्ध करुन घ्यावयाची आहेत. उपलब्ध होणाऱ्या कलमा/रोपांचे नियोजन, त्यांचे वितरण या बाबतच्या सविस्तर सूचना संचालक (फलो.), कृषि आयुक्तालय हे सर्व संबंधितांना निर्गमित करतील.

३. <u>लागवड मर्यादा</u> :

या योजनेचा फायदा जट्रोफाची किमान १०० किंवा जास्तीत जास्त २२०० झाडांची लागवड करणाऱ्या वैयक्तिक लाभार्थींना देण्यात येईल.

४. जट्रोफा लागवड योजनेंतर्गत प्रती झाड रु.१८.४० एवढे अनुदान ३ वर्षाच्या कालावधीकरिता देय होईल व अनुदानाचे वाटप प्रती झाड प्रथम वर्षी रु.९.२० दुस-या वर्षी रु.५.५० आणि तिस-या वर्षी रु.३.७० या प्रमाणात अदा करण्यात येईल. ज्या लाभार्थ्यांची दुस-या वर्षी ७५ टक्के व तिस-या वर्षी ९० टक्के झाडे जिवंत असतील त्या लाभार्थ्यांना दुस-या / तिस-या वर्षाचे अनुदान देय राहील.

५. उपरोल्लिखीत अ.क्र.१ येथील दि.२७.६.२००५च्या शासन निर्णयातील परि.६ मध्ये योजना राबविण्याकरिता मार्गदर्शक सूचना या शिर्षाखाली ज्या विविध परिशिष्टांचा/प्रपत्रांचा उल्लेख करण्यात आला आहे व त्यामध्ये उपरोल्लिखीत अ.क्र.२ येथील दि.२४.११.२००५ च्या शासन निर्णयान्वये केलेल्या सुधारणा विचारात घेऊन ती परिशिष्टे/प्रपत्रे योग्य तो बदल करुन जट्रोफा लागवडीचा कार्यक्रम राबविण्यासाठी स्वतंत्रपणे निर्गमित करण्याकरिता संचालक फलोत्पादन यांना प्राधिकृत करण्यात येत आहे.

६. जत्रोफा बियांच्या खरेदीबाबत किंवा उत्पन्नाबाबत शासनाची कोणतीही जबाबदारी राहणार नाही.

हे आदेश नियोजन विभाग (रोहयो), नियोजन विभाग (का.-१४४३) व वित्त विभागाच्या सहमतीने व वित्त विभागाचा अनौपचारिक संदर्भ क्र.१४३/व्यय-१ दि.१९.४.२००६ अन्वये निर्गमित करण्यात येत आहे.

महाराष्ट्राचे राज्यपाल यांच्या आदेशानुसार व नावाने

(वि.म.कोकणे)
सह सचिव, महाराष्ट्र शासन

प्रति,
मा. मुख्यमंत्री यांचे प्रधान सचिव
मा. मंत्री फलोत्पादन यांचे खाजगी सचिव
मा. मंत्री (रोहयो) यांचे खाजगी सचिव / मा. मंत्री (कृषि) यांचे खाजगी सचिव
मा. राज्यमंत्री (फलोत्पादन) / मा. राज्यमंत्री (कृषि व रोहयो) यांचे खाजगी सचिव
सर्व विभागीय आयुक्त
सर्व कुलगुरु (कृषि विद्यापीठ)
आयुक्त कृषि, महाराष्ट्र राज्य, पुणे
संचालक फलोत्पादन, महाराष्ट्र राज्य, पुणे (१५ जादा प्रतीसह)
सर्व जिल्हाधिकारी
सर्व मुख्य कार्यकारी अधिकारी, जिल्हा परिषद
सर्व विभागीय कृषि सह संचालक
सर्व जिल्हा अधिक्षक कृषि अधिकारी
सर्व उपविभागीय कृषि अधिकारी / सर्व जिल्हा परिषदाचे कृषि विकास अधिकारी
सर्व तालुका कृषि अधिकारी
महालेखापाल, महाराष्ट्र-१ / २ (लेखा व अनुज्ञेयता/लेखा परिक्षा) मुंबई/नागपूर
सर्व जिल्हा कोषागार अधिकारी,
वित्त विभाग, मत्रालय, मुंबई (व्यय-१)
नियोजन विभाग, कार्यासन-(१४४३) / (रोहयो-१०), मंत्रालय, मुंबई
ग्राम विकास व जल संधारण विभाग, मंत्रालय, मुंबई/ आदिवासी विकास विभाग, मंत्रालय,मुंबई
महसूल व वनविभाग (महसूल), मंत्रालय, मुंबई
सहसचिव/उपसचिव/अवर सचिव (कृषि व फलोत्पादन) कृषि व पदुम विभाग.
सर्व कार्यासने कृषि व पदुम विभाग
निवड नस्ती

Bibliography

Books

Agarwal, Bina: *A Field of One's Own, Gender and Land Rights in South Asia*, Cambridge University Press, New Delhi, 1994.

Bhatt, Anil: *Development and Social Justice*, Sage Publications, New Delhi, 1989.

Bhatt, Ashish: Voluntary Organisations and Tribal Development in Madhya Pradesh, in Sah, D.C. and Sisodia, Yatindra Singh, *Tribal Issues in India*, Rawat Publications, Jaipur, 2004.

Bokil, Milind: *Katkari Vikas Ki Visthapan*? Mauj Prakashan, Mumbai, 2006.

Bobo, Kim, Kendell, Jackie and Max, Steve: *Organising for Social Change*, Seven Locks Publications, Washington, 1991.

Centre for Development and Human Rights: *The Right to Development: A Primer*, Sage Publications, New Delhi, 2004.

Corbridge, Stewart: *Development Studies*, Arnold Publications, London, 1995.

Crowell, Daniel W.: *The SEWA Movement and Rural Development*, Sage Publications, New Delhi, 2003.

Dantwala, M.L.: Promises To Keep, in Dantwala, M.L., Sethi, Harsh and Visaria, Pravin (eds.), *Social Change Through Voluntary Action*, Sage Publications, New Delhi, 1998.

Desai, A.R.: *Rural Sociology in India*, Popular Publications, Mumbai, 1969.

Deshpande, V.V.: NGOs and Development, in Pawar, S.N., et al, Rawat Publications, Jaipur, 2004.

Deshpande, Vasant: *Adivasis of Thane*, Dastane Publications, Pune, 1985.

Dhanagare, D.N.: *Themes and Perspectives in Indian Sociology*, Rawat Publications, New Delhi, 1993.

Doshi, S.L. and Jain, P.C.: *Rural Sociology*, Rawat Publications, Jaipur, 1999.

Dube, S.C.: *Development Perspectives for the 1980s*, Abhinav Publications, New Delhi, 1983.

Farnandes, Walter: *Social Activists and People's Movements*, Indian Social Institute, New Delhi, 1985.

Freire, Paulo: *Pedagogy of the Oppressed*, Penguin, Harmondsworth, 1996.

Gandhi, M.K.: *An Autobiography or The Story of My Experiments with Truth*, Navajivan Publishing House, Ahmedabad, April, 2001.

Gare, Govind: *Adivasi Sahitya Sammelan Adhyakshaiya Bhashane*, Sugava Prakashan, Pune, 2005.

Heredia, Rudolf: *Tribal Education for Community Development, A Study of Schooling in the Talasari Mission Area*, Concept Publishing Company, New Delhi, 1992.

Indian Council of Social Welfare: *Social Development and Voluntary Action*, Bombay, 1973.

Jain, R.B.: NGOs as the Non-State Actor in Public Administration, in *Public Administration in India*, Deep and Deep, New Delhi, 2002.

Kaushik, Pitambar Datt: Ambedkar-Prophet of Self-Help and Saviour of Untouchables, in *Bhimrao Ramji Ambedkar: A Biography of His Vision and Ideas*, edited by Grover, Verinder, Deep & Deep Publications, New Delhi, 1998.

Keer, Dhananjay: *Dr. Babasaheb Ambedkar (Marathi: Biography)*, Popular Prakashan, Mumbai, 2006.

Kulkarni, Sharad: *Tribal Communities in Maharashtra, Struggles for Survival*, National Centre for Advocacy Studies, Pune, 2002.

Lawani, B.T.: *NGOs in Development*, Rawat Publications, Jaipur, 1999.

Louis, Prakash: Disempowering Masses, The Scheduled Tribes, *Alternative Economic Survey of India, 2005-2006*, Danish Books, Delhi, 2006.

Mander, Harsh: *Tribal Policy: Pulling Back from the Brink*? Multiplexus Press, New Delhi, 2004.

Misra, R.P.: *Development Issues of Our Times*, Concept Publishing Company, New Delhi, 1995.

Mohanty, Manoranjan and Singh, Anil K.: *Voluntarism and Government*, Voluntary Action Network India, New Delhi, 2001.

Mukherjee, Rudrangshu: *The Penguin Gandhi Reader*, Penguin Books, New Delhi, 1993.

Pandey, Rajendra: *Modernisation and Social Change*, Criterion Publications, New Delhi, 1988.

Pandey, Shashi Ranjan: *Community Action for Social Justice*, Sage Publications, New Delhi, 1991.

Pandit, Vivek: *Prevention of Atrocities*, Vidhayak Sansad Publications, Thane, 1995.

Pandit, Vivek: *Fearless Minds*, National Centre for Advocacy Studies, Pune, 2000.

Parikh, Kirit and Radhakrishna: *India Development Report, 2004-05*, Oxford University Press, New Delhi, 2005.

Parulekar, Godavari: *Jevha Manoos Jaga Hoto*, Mauj Prakashan, Mumbai, 1999.

Pawar, S.N., Ambekar, J.B. and Shrikant, D.: *NGOs and Development*, Rawat Publications, Jaipur, 2004.

Ramagundam, Rahul: *Defeated Innocence*, Grassroots India Publishers, New Delhi, 2001.

Robin Lal: *The Dynamics of NGOs*, Dominant Publishers and Distributors, New Delhi, 2004.

Sah, D.C.: Partnership Ethics and Environmental Politics, in Sah, D.C, and Sisodia, Yatindra Singh, *Tribal Issues in India*, Rawat Publications, Jaipur, 2004.

Samuel, John: *Social Action: An Indian Panorama*, VANI, New Delhi, 2000.

Sen, Amartya: *Development As Freedom*, Oxford University Press, New Delhi, 1999.

Shah, Ghanshyam: *Social Movements in India, Tribal Movements*, Sage Publications, New Delhi, 2005.

Singh, Amar Kumar and Jabbi, M.K: *Tribals in India*, Har-Anand Publications, New Delhi, 1995.

Singh, K.S.: *The Scheduled Tribes*, Oxford University Press, Calcutta, 1994.

Sommer, John G.: *Empowering the Oppressed*, Sage Publications, New Delhi, 2001.

Sooryamoorthy, R. and Gangrade, K.D.: *NGOs in India*, Rawat Publications, New Delhi, 2006.

Tagore, Rabindranath: *Gitanjali*, Full Circle Publishing (A Division of Hind Pocket Books Pvt. Ltd.), Delhi, 2002.

Thakur, Ashutosh: *Tribal Development and its Paradoxes*, Authors Press, New Delhi, 2001.

Vakil, A.K: Political Socialisation of Scheduled Castes and Dr. Ambedkar, in *Bhimrao Ramji Ambedkar: A Biography of His Vision and Ideas*, edited by Grover, Verinder, Deep & Deep Publications, New Delhi, 1998.

Articles in Journals

Banu, Shareen C.P.: The Substantive Democracy; Role of Civil Society in Rural Karnataka, *Indian Anthropologist*, Vol. 33, No. 2, 2003.

Baviskar, B.S.: NGOs and Civil Society in India, *Sociological Bulletin*, 50 (1), March, 2001.

Dalvi, Surekha and Bokil, Milind: In Search of Justice, Tribal Communities and Land Rights in Costal Maharashtra, *Economic and Political Weekly*, August 5, 2000.

Joshi, Satyakam: State, Forest and Tribal Rights; The Case of Dangs Tribals, *Man & Development*, September 2000.

Joshi, Seema: Impact of Economic Reforms on Social Sector Expenditure in India, *Economic and Political Weekly*, January 28, 2006.

Kothari, Rajni: The Non-Party Political Process, *Economic and Political Weekly*, February 4, 1984.

Kumar, Raj: Capacity Building of Panchayats for Rural Development: Some Emerging Areas for NGOs, *Man & Development*, March 2002.

Panda, Biswambhar and Pattanaik, Binay Kumar: Effectiveness of Grassroots NGOs, *Man & Development*, June 2005.

Saldanha, Munshi Indra: Tribal Women in the Warli Revolt: 1945-47, *Economic and Political Weekly*, Vol. XXI, No. 17, *Review of Women's Studies*, 26 April 1986.

Saldanha, Munshi Indra: Attached Labour in Thane, *Economic and Political Weekly*, May 20, 1989.

Sharma, S.L.: Social Development, 'Reflections on the Concept and the Indian Experience', *Guru Nanak Journal of Sociology*, Vol. 10, Nos. 1-2, April-October 1989.

Sinha, Archana: Economic Empowerment and Amelioration of Tribals in India, *Kurukshetra*, Vol. 54, No. 9, July 2006.

Srivastava, S.S. and Tandon, Rajesh: How Large Is India's Non-Profit Sector? *Economic and Political Weekly*, 7 May 2005.

Tilak, Jandhyala B.G.: Role of NGOs in Education in India, *Man & Development*, June 2004.

Articles in Bulletin

Behar, Amitabh: *Civil Society Voices*, New Delhi, March 2005.

Articles on Website

www. http://go.worldbank.org/WXKIV52RBO

Articles and News in Newspapers

Correspondent: Maharashtra Plans to Start Open Schools for Dropouts, *The Mumbai Age*, August 15, 2000.

Das, Arun Kumar: First National Policy on Voluntary Sector Awaits Cabinet Approval, *Sunday Times of India*, Pune, July 9, 2006.

Mishra, Neeraj: The Noose Tightens, *India Today*, New Delhi, January 29, 2007.

Reporter: Ganeshpuri Aasharamatil Majuranchi Marhanichi Takrar, *Maharashtra Times*, April 23, 1987.

Root, Vidya Nayak: Freed... At last, *Indian Express*, Bombay, December 23, 1986.

Root, Vidya Nayak: Broken Bonds, *Indian Express*, Bombay , May 10, 1987.

Special Reporter: Virarmadhil Pach Vethbigaranchi Sutka, *Mumbai Sakal*, October 14, 1982.

Special Reporter: Sadicholi Pach Mann Bhatasathi Bavis Varshe Vethbigari, *Maharashtra Times*, August 18, 1982.

Special Reporter: Vethbigar Samasyechi Pahani and Vethbigar Adivasi Charitarhartas Lagale, *Maharashtra Times*, July 13, 1984.

Special Reporter: Vasai Talukayat Char Pidhaya Vethbeegari Karnaraya Tevis Vethbeegaranchi Mukatata, *Mumbai Sakal*, December 19, 1986.

Reports

Bhoir, Balarm: *Annual Report-1999*, Shramjeevi Sanghatana, Thane, 1999.

Bhoir, Balaram: *Annual Report, 2005-06*, Shramjeevi Sanghatana, Usgaon Dongari, Thane, 2007.

Bhoir, Balaram: *Chitramay Itihas Shramjeevi Sanghatana, 1982-2007*, Shramjeevi Sanghatana, Thane, 21, October 2007.

Cohen, David: *The Elements of Advocacy in Resource Kit for Advocacy and Campaign building*, National Centre for Advocacy Studies, Pune, 1996.

Goswami, Paromita: *Taking Roots-Spreading Wings*, Vidhayak Sansad and Shramjeevi Sanghatana, Thane, October 20, 1996.

Government of India: *Maharashtra Development Report*, Planning Commission, Government of India, Academic Foundation, New Delhi, 2007.

Government of India: Ministry of Agriculture, National Commission on Farmers, *Draft National Policy for Farmers*, New Delhi, April 13, 2006.

Government of India: Ministry of Tribal Affairs, *Draft National Tribal Policy*, New Delhi, July 5, 2006.

Government of India: Ministry of Tribal Affairs, *Programmes for Promotion of Voluntary Action, Annual Report 2005-06*, New Delhi, 2006.

Government of India: Ministry of Tribal Affairs, *Scheduled Tribes and Scheduled Areas, Annual Report 2003-2004*, New Delhi, 2003-2004.

Government of India: Ministry of Welfare, *Report of the Working Group on Development and Welfare of Scheduled Tribes during the Eighth Five Year Plan, 1990-95*, New Delhi, November, 1989.

Government of India: *National Policy on the Voluntary Sector*, Planning Commission, May 2007.

Government of India: *Report of the Commissioner for Scheduled Castes and Scheduled Tribes*, New Delhi, Twenty Ninth Report, 1987-89.

Government of India: *Tenth Five Year Plan*, New Delhi, 2002-07.

Government of Maharashtra: *Adivasi Vikas Parichay*, Commission for Tribal Development, Government Press, Mumbai, 2003-04.

Government of Maharashtra: *Census of India 1981; District Census Handbook Thane,* Government Printing Press, Bombay, 1986.

Government of Maharashtra: *Child Death Evaluation Committee, Second & Final Report*, Family Welfare Department, Pune, March 24, 2005.

Government of Maharashtra: Department of Agriculture, Animal Husbandry, Milk Production and Fishery Development, *Government Resolution*, Mantralaya, Mumbai, April 26, 2006.

Government of Maharashtra: *Development of Tribals*, Tribal Development Department, Government Press, Mumbai, 1992.

Government of Maharashtra: *Gazetteer of the Bombay Presidency, Thana places of Interest*, Gazetteers Department, Bombay, 2000.

Jain, Navinchandra and Tribhuwan, Robin: *An Overview of Tribal Research Studies, Demographic Profile of Tribals in India with Special Reference to Maharashtra,* Tribal Research and Training Institute, Government of Maharashtra, Pune, 1995.

Jayachandran, Usha: *Vidhayak Sansad's Bhonga Shalas; Bringing Schools to Tribal Migrant Children: A Case Study*, January 10, 2004.

Mahajan, Kavita: *Parivartnachaya Prakriyecha Jeetajagata Purava*, Vidhayak Sansad and Shramjeevi Sanghatana, Thane, 1998.

National Centre for Advocacy Studies: *Draft Paper on Understanding Advocacy*, Pune, 2006.

Pandit, Vidyullata: *Annual Report 2007*, Shramjeevi Sanghatana, Thane, 2007.

Pandit, Vidyullata: *Annual Report, 2006-07*,Vidhayak, Sansad, Usgaon Dongari, Thane, 2007.

Pandit, Vidyullatta: *Ropya Mahostav Visheshank*, Shramjeevi Sanghatana, Thane, October 2007.

Pandit, Vidyullata: *Shramjeevi Sanghatana Annual Report-2003*, Shramjeevi Sanghatana, Thane, 2004.

Pandit, Vivek: *Samarthan Vartapatra*, Samarthan, Mumbai, July, 2000.

Samarthan: *Budget Maharashtra State 2006-07*, Centre for Budget Studies, Mumbai, 2006.

Securing Rights: *Citizens Report on Millennium Development Goals*, Books for Change, Bangalore, 2005.

Shramjeevi Sanghatana: *Annual Report-2005*, Usgaon Dongari, Thane, 2006.